REAL FOOD
REAL EASY

120 Recipes Made Fast with Only a Handful of Simple, Fresh Ingredients

GEORGE STELLA

with Christian Stella

dĤ

DYNAMIC HOUSEWARES INC

First paperback edition 2010

10 9 8 7 6 5 4 3

For information about special discounts for bulk purchases
please contact sales@dynamichousewares.com

Please consult your physician before making any
drastic changes to the way you eat.

Authors: George Stella with Christian Stella

Book design, food photographs and illustrations: Christian and Elise Stella
with Stella Star Designs LLC

Assistant Editor: Kelly Machamer

Manufactured in the USA

ISBN 978-0-9841887-2-7

I dedicate this book to my family, who worked really hard
(and ate a lot of good food!) to make this book a reality.

Table of Contents

Introduction

If you were to look back at me when I was at my heaviest weight of 467 pounds, I'm sure that one of the first questions that you would have wanted to ask was, "George, how did you get to be this way?" Sure, I probably could have given you numerous examples of choices I had made to help get me to that point. I probably would have told you about the times where I found myself home after a long grueling day of working in a restaurant kitchen, and the first thing I would do is eat whatever I could eat to make up for a day of missed meals. Famished, I would find myself eating a combination of leftovers, snack foods, and sugary processed desserts. It really didn't matter, as long as I ate as much as possible, as quickly as possible, after a day of practically fasting. Though I can think of many specific moments of poor food related decisions, it was our overall lifestyle that was killing not only me but my family as well.

My name is George Stella, and yes, at one point I was well on my way to weighing 500 pounds! Add in my wife Rachel, who at one point weighed 205 pounds, my oldest son Anthony, who weighed 225 pounds, and my youngest son Christian, at 305 pounds, and you have a single family of four that weighed over half a ton!

Understandably, I am not exaggerating when I say that the way we were eating was indeed killing us. Looking back at the years in which we were literally growing together as a family,

I remember our meals consisting on average of things ranging from pizza and macaroni and cheese, to Chinese and fast food. To us then, these foods were easily obtained and readily available. The problem was that the more that we ate these foods, the more weight we gained, and the less motivated and physically able we were to cook our own meals. Being a chef, I've always loved to cook, especially for those I love. Unfortunately, the larger I grew, the more difficult it was to stand long enough to prepare home cooked meals. It actually got to the point that I had to cook meals while sitting in an office chair, wheeling from the fridge to the stove!

Our situation was certainly bad, and quickly on its way to getting much worse. At 25 years old and 300 pounds, I experienced my first heart attack. Years later, at my heaviest, I had a doctor look me right in the eyes and tell me that I was going to die, because my heart could not continue to supply my extra weight with enough blood to keep it going. With my sons still being in their teens, and Rachel slowly gaining weight after years of being the "slender" one of our family, their health was not in as immediate of danger as my own, but I knew that they were clearly on the same path and not too far behind.

Top left: Video still of Rachel at over 200 pounds, sitting with George.

Top right: George at 467 pounds.

Bottom: Rachel and George today.

Stella Style

It was our overall lifestyle that brought us to the weight we were at, but we were convinced that we could find some quick fix. In the beginning and in desperation, it was a diet plan we were searching for, even though we had never found one that worked for us. After everyone in my family unsuccessfully tried all sorts of diet plans, I was doubtful that we would ever find something that would replace the lifestyle we had fallen into. Any changes in our life needed to be something that would not only help us to live, but be something that we could live with. Otherwise, we seemed sure to fail as we had in the past. What we didn't realize was that it was all about the mindset we were in. That a "diet" is something you do temporarily and with constant thinking, over-thinking, and effort; what we needed was something that would just come as second nature for us for the rest of our lives.

What finally worked for us was a lifestyle initially based on Dr. Atkins' diet, which centers around drastically limiting your carb intake. In the beginning, this seemed to be the perfect change for us, as limiting the amount of food we ate was not as important as limiting the amount of carbs. After a while, we did find that we were all missing the old comfort foods that we had gotten used to over the years, and so Stella Style was created. Simply put, Stella Style was our making the low carb lifestyle work to fit our tastes, rather than restricting ourselves completely in order to follow a plan created by someone else.

What worked for us, worked extremely well, with our family losing over 560 pounds. Rachel and Anthony both lost over 70 pounds, and Christian and I both lost over half of our body weight with 160 pounds and 265 pounds gone respectively. I've told this story dozens of times now, but I will never get tired of telling it—as each time I do, I get letters from people all over the country who take back their own family's health and make the changes they need to make for themselves—and it is truly as inspiring to me as I am sure our family's story is to them.

In essence, we found that losing weight had more to do with learning about ingredients, foods, and how to better prepare them, than following any strict set of rules. We learned that we couldn't let counting each and every carbohydrate or calorie rule our lives or we would tire of having to work, just to eat and live. Instead, we just spent the first few months of our weight loss learning what foods were the healthiest and then moved on with our lives, eating as many of those foods as possible. At the same time, we learned which foods were the unhealthiest, and made the decision to avoid them from then on. Foods like trans-fats, white flour, and sugar or corn syrup. You'd be surprised the weight many have lost just by making the decision to avoid high fructose corn syrup, which is used to sweeten soda and a large percentage of processed foods.

I have always said that you need to like what you are eating, or you are dooming yourself to failure. For this reason, it is incredibly important that what you're eating includes foods you enjoy! For us, Stella Style is not only eating fresh foods that we love, but using those fresh foods to re-create our old favorites in a healthier way. Getting into your kitchen is key! You have to stop and realize that cooking a home cooked meal from fresh ingredients can be just as easy as cooking from a box and just as fast as ordering a pizza, as long as you know what to do!

As my family and I, and therefore our version of Stella Style has evolved, so have my books. My previous books are focused more on utilizing foods that are simply low in carbs, but as the weight dropped off, we started enjoying more and more of what are known as "good carbs" like whole grains and legumes. I've learned that I can't give the perfect answer for each individual to lose weight, as every individual is different; I can only share with you our story and our family recipes featuring the fresh foods that we like to eat to stay healthy.

I firmly believe that whether you are experiencing difficulties with your weight, are diabetic, have gluten allergies or intolerances, or you simply want to follow a healthy lifestyle that makes you feel good, most of these recipes, if not all (depending on your circumstances) can help. Not to mention, they are made up of pure and fresh flavors that you and your family are sure to love!

Simple, Fresh and Full of Flavor

When I set out to make this book, I wanted to write healthy and delicious recipes that were simple, easy, and in 5 or less ingredients. So hey, 2 out of 3 ain't bad! I've seen many 5 ingredient cookbooks in bookstores and figured that it was the perfect idea for my next book as I always try to make my recipes inexpensive and easy, and fewer ingredients means fewer costs. Simple, delicious food is food you'll want to make over and over again.

I began this undertaking by going through our massive collection of family recipes and pulling the best ones that also happened to have less ingredients. It was not long before I realized that limiting the book to a set number of ingredients wasn't my style at all. I have been a chef all of my life, and I simply cannot sacrifice the flavor of a dish in order to give my book a catchy gimmick. Looking through other examples of 5 ingredient or less cookbooks, I found that many recipes seemed to have cut simple seasonings like salt, pepper, or garlic powder, just to stay under the limit. I also found that they would use too many pre-packaged mixes and/or processed foods and cans of soup to keep the number of ingredients down, and this certainly goes against my belief of food being fresh and made from scratch!

You will find that there are still many recipes in this book that certainly include 5 or even less ingredients, but you will also find recipes with more than 5 ingredients. If you look closely at the ingredient lists for the recipes with more ingredients, you will often find that you have many of the items in your spice cabinet and pantry. So while I can't make the promise of 5 ingredients or less for every recipe in this book, I can promise that your shopping list will be small and inexpensive, and that your meals will be well seasoned and made from fresh foods!

On the next page, I have included a pantry list of basic items that I use often in the recipes in this book and that are good to have on hand, keeping your shopping lists shorter in the future.

Pantry List

Use this list to help stock your pantry with many of the items used frequently throughout the book. By no means do you have to have or purchase everything on this list to get cooking, but the more you have beforehand, the merrier! With a well stocked pantry, we found while re-testing all of our recipes that pretty much all of the recipes in this book can be made for less than $15.

salt	balsamic vinegar
pepper	white vinegar
garlic powder	cider vinegar
onion powder	white wine vinegar
thyme	lemon juice
bay leaves	grated Parmesan cheese
cayenne pepper	Dijon mustard
oregano	light mayonnaise
sage	whole wheat flour
poultry seasoning	soy flour
Italian seasoning	almond flour
paprika	bulk sugar substitute
chili powder	trans-fat free margarine
ground cinnamon	eggs
nutmeg	heavy cream
vanilla extract	half and half
soy sauce	unsweetened soy milk
teriyaki sauce	baking soda
olive oil	baking powder
vegetable oil	unsweetened baking chocolate
sesame oil	fresh herbs

"Good Carbs"

The thing that was most in common between all of our favorite meals back when we were struggling with our weights was that they were often made up of processed foods high in calories and with little nutritional value. The key for us at the time was that they were cheap, quick, and easy. We didn't consider that these foods were comprised primarily of carbohydrates, and not just any carbs, but what we call "bad carbs." As you will see by my recipes in this book that include fruits, whole grains, and an assortment of vegetables of all types, there are carbs that can be considered "good carbs" as well. Rather than concerning myself with counting carbs, I now focus solely on whether or not the foods that I am eating are comprised of good carbs.

As I've mentioned, fruits, vegetables, and whole grains are all examples of good carbs, but there are definitely some that are lower in sugar and other carbs, and are therefore better than others.

I have included lists of which fresh foods are the lowest in carbs and which are the highest, as well as a list of what I consider to be the most nutritious whole grains, nuts, seeds, and legumes. Finally, I have compiled a short list of the bad carbs that you should try to avoid whenever possible. These lists are by no means exhaustive, but include many common choices.

BEST (LOWEST) CARB VEGETABLES

mushrooms
celery
radishes
asparagus
broccoli
eggplant
bell peppers
artichokes
lettuce
cucumber
green beans
spinach
collard greens
cauliflower
cabbage
zucchini
yellow squash
spaghetti squash
snap peas

GOOD (MEDIUM) CARB VEGETABLES

sweet potatoes
pumpkins
sweet onions

HIGHEST CARB VEGETABLES

corn
peas
beets
carrots
lima beans
parsnips

Best (lowest) Carb Fruits

raspberries
cranberries
blackberries
blueberries
strawberries
cantaloupe
honeydew
rhubarb
lemons
limes
citrus zest
tomatoes
coconut

Good (medium) Carb Fruits

peaches
apples
nectarines
kiwis
figs

Highest Carb Fruits

bananas
oranges
tangerines
grapes
cherries
mangoes
pomegranates
pineapple
watermelon
dried fruit

Good Nuts, Seeds, and Legumes

almonds
walnuts
pecans
cashews
macadamias

pine nuts
hazelnuts
pistachios
peanuts
lentils
chickpeas
soybeans
sunflower seeds
pumpkin seeds

Nutritious Whole Grains

whole wheat
whole oats
popcorn
quinoa
bulgur
whole rye
spelt
barley
millet
wheat germ
wild rice (not pilaf)

The "Bad" Stuff

white sugar
brown sugar
corn syrup
white flour
white or red potatoes
trans-fat
(partially hydrogenated oil)

Top three: Christian, before and after
Bottom three: Anthony, before and after

Whole Grains

As far as carbs go, whole grains with their many health benefits and the way in which they are metabolized by the body, can certainly be considered a good carb. What makes a whole grain a whole grain is the fact that it consists of the entire parts of the grain, unprocessed. Most of the nutritional parts and fiber are stripped away in processing to make bad carbs such as white flour. You will want to check packages and the ingredients list carefully when buying items you believe to be whole grain to be sure that they are in fact 100% whole grain, as many packages can claim they are whole grain if only a portion of the ingredients in them are.

The most basic thing to know about whole grains is that they are digested by your body differently than processed simple (bad) carbs. I am not a doctor or nutritionist, so I can only shed so much light onto this, but in essence, good carbs digest slower and less of the good carbs you eat are converted to sugar and then fat in your body.

When my family and I first started losing weight we did not include any whole grains. While they are a good carb, they are still a carb, and at the time we were eating foods that were the lowest in carbs to really help us shed the massive amount of weight we had to lose. As we lost more and more weight, we were able to start eating various good carbs and create our own style, Stella Style. So while I do not necessarily recommend whole grains in the beginning if you have a large amount of weight to lose, they can be or become a great addition to a healthy, good carb lifestyle! To this day, even though I use whole wheat flour from time to time, I still use other flours, such as soy and almond flour, when they are the best ingredient for the recipe. I have done my best to keep most whole grains to their own category in this book, so that you can decide if they are right for you.

Reduced Fat Dairy

Other than milk, which is somewhat high in natural sugars, my family has enjoyed all sorts of dairy products throughout our weight loss. While we were once very staunch advocates of eating the regular, full fat versions of dairy products, and had no problem losing weight doing so, our stance on low fat options has changed since I released my first book.

When I released my first book, almost all low-fat dairy products contained added sugar, but over the years, many of them have been reformulated and the sugar removed. Now they are not only lower in carbs than they used to be, but also far, far better tasting, without the sweet aftertaste they used to have. I will

admit that I had been a holdout on the low-fat dairy, afraid to change what was working for me, even as I watched Christian eat it every day as he effortlessly lost the last 80 pounds of his weight loss.

You will now find that I have used low-fat cream cheese and sour cream almost exclusively throughout the book, but you are more than welcome to substitute for the full fat versions if that is what you prefer. I base my choice of whether I use a full-fat or a low-fat version of an ingredient on whether it complements the dish and will not use low-fat if I believe it will compromise the texture or flavor. As a rule, I typically still do not suggest reduced fat shredded cheeses, because they melt poorly and in general don't taste as good as the regular, but you are welcome to use them in any recipe, if you prefer. I have also found that most *fat-free* dairy still contains too much added sugars to recommend.

Specialty Ingredients

Though I have tried to keep the recipes in this book as simple as possible for everyone to enjoy, these three ingredients might be tricky to find without an explanation.

Almond Flour

Almond flour can be found in some health food markets like Whole Foods, but we like to make our own, as it is usually cheaper. To make almond flour: simply grind raw almonds (sold in the baking aisle) in a food processor until they are a finely granulated consistency. Some recipes in this book also call for almond flour made from blanched almond slivers to give baked goods a cleaner, whiter look. Regular almonds ground into almond flour will work fine in those recipes if that is all you have on hand.

Bulk Sugar Substitute

Nearly all no calorie sweetener in this book is listed as "bulk sugar substitute". By bulk sugar substitute, we mean a sweetener that measures cup for cup the same as white sugar. Single serving packets of sweetener will not work! They are far more concentrated than the stuff that comes in a bag. We prefer to buy the big bags of Splenda, as it doesn't lose its sweetness when baking, but be careful that you don't accidentally buy the bags of Splenda that are mixed with an equal amount of real brown sugar. Splenda has always worked best for us, but if you enjoy another no calorie sweetener that stays sweet when cooked (there seems to be a lot of sweeteners popping up these days), please feel free to use what you prefer.

Soy Flour

Soy flour is just very low carb flour made from soybeans. It is sold in almost all of the major grocery chains now, usually in the organic or healthy eating section, but sometimes just in the ordinary flour section.

Tips for an Affordable Good Carb Lifestyle

Back before my family and I lost our weight, the way we were eating was almost entirely based on foods that seemed to be a great value for the money. Sadly, processed junk food looks to be the best value in the grocery store when you are not considering how unfulfilling and hungry it leaves you only a short time later. We all better realize now that fresh, healthy eating does not have to cost more! It is my hope that you will find that the recipes in this book are not only delicious, fresh, and easy, but that they are also affordable.

As I've previously said, my biggest goal for this book is to keep your grocery lists short. Naturally, this will help keep grocery costs down in itself, but I wanted to also include a list of tips that I have found helpful in maintaining an affordable good carb lifestyle.

Grow Your Own Fruits, Vegetables, and Herbs

Rachel has maintained a garden at our house for years, and we have all greatly enjoyed the fresh fruits and vegetables that she has provided! Besides great fresh flavors, your own garden has other benefits. For one, it is a rewarding way to get outside and get some exercise. Also, letting your children watch and/or get involved in the growing process helps to get them excited about eating fruits and vegetables (that usually taste even better than the grocer's produce section). Of course, the most obvious benefit is that the cost of the

seeds or starter plants is much cheaper than buying produce from a grocery store. Often times, you can buy an already maturing fresh herb plant in a pot of soil for under $3, the same price you would pay for a small package of the herb in the refrigerated case. Even if you're not as vigilant as Rachel about watering the herbs, they should still last longer than the cut and packaged herbs. With a little more care, they

cook in bulk on your day off so that you have no worries during the week.

Finally, one of the best things about having a freezer is that you are able to fill it with frozen vegetables (the ones you haven't already grown in your own garden of course). Frozen vegetables are delicious, often cheaper than fresh, and still very nutritious! While I prefer cooking with fresh vegetables, I often keep my freezer stocked with bags of frozen, in the same manner that I keep my spice cabinet stocked with different spices. You never know what you're going to need!

GET THE MOST OUT OF THIS BOOK

With each recipe including extensive tips and "variations", I hope this book will not only present you with a great value, but will encourage you to create more than just the recipes as they are written. Consider this book a book of methods, rather than recipes, and you will be able to create more great meals than could ever fit between these pages. I've tried to cover a wide variety of ingredients, as well as cuisines in this book to give you all the tools (or methods) you need to create your own recipes, or at least re-create old favorites in a healthier way.

Cooking should be fun, creative, and about you and your family. I created Stella Style along with *my* family, and I just know that by following and altering these simple, yet fulfilling recipes, you will be well on your way to finding the style that fits you and your family!

will quadruple in size and keep you in fresh herbs all year long. With a food dehydrator or an oven on the lowest, warm setting, you can even dry fresh herbs to make jarred spices that will last for up to 2 years.

GET THE MOST OUT OF YOUR FREEZER

Used effectively, your freezer can be one of your best tools when trying to maintain an affordable healthy lifestyle! With your freezer, you can buy in bulk and freeze what you are not ready to use immediately. This allows you to take great advantage of specials and coupons as they become available, and also allows you to shop at larger bulk club stores.

Along the same lines of buying in bulk, I find that *cooking* in bulk and freezing what you don't eat to be another great trick. This I find is a great solution if you work long days that make cooking every night difficult. You can

Starters and Snacks

prep time 10 mins	cook time 60 mins	serves 12

Baked Garlic Wings

calories: 320 | fat: 14g | protein: 45g | fiber: 0g | NET CARBS: **0.5g**

I bake chicken wings all the time, as I can get the freshest, cheapest wings from a Puerto Rican specialty supermarket a few miles from our house. It's very hard to find real, fresh wings without water added to them in the packaging process these days (the less water added, the crispier the wings will be), but the smaller butchers and markets that package them themselves are usually the best bet. These wings bake up crispy and remind me of fresh, hot garlic bread when you're eating them.

Shopping List

4 pounds fresh **chicken wings**
2 tablespoons **olive oil**
2 ½ tablespoons **minced garlic**
1 teaspoon **garlic powder**
1 teaspoon **salt**
½ teaspoon **black pepper**
¼ cup grated **Parmesan cheese**

1. Place oven rack in the center position and preheat to 375 degrees.

2. In a large bowl, combine the chicken wings, olive oil, minced garlic, garlic powder, salt, and black pepper and toss all to coat.

3. Place the coated wings on a sheet pan and bake for 1 hour, or until skin becomes crispy.

4. Sprinkle baked wings with Parmesan cheese while still hot, shaking wings around pan to evenly coat all. Serve immediately.

George's Tips | Line the sheet pan with heavy duty aluminum foil before baking, for an easier clean up. You should still wash the pan, but you definitely won't need to scrub.

Variation | Skip the Parmesan cheese, and try tossing the baked garlic wings in 2 tablespoons of honey before serving for delicious Honey Garlic Wings! Add a pinch of ground cayenne pepper for a little spice to offset the sweet honey.

prep time	cook time	serves
15 mins	20 mins	8

Tempura Asparagus

calories: 200 | fat: 16g | protein: 8g | fiber: 2.5g | NET CARBS: **5g**

This appetizer is worthy of being served in an upscale restaurant, though it is deceptively easy to make. You could never guess that the tempura batter is made without any white flour. I like it best with the dipping sauce recipe at the bottom of the page!

1. Place a pot over medium-high heat and fill with at least 2 inches of vegetable oil. Heat oil until 350 degrees, about 5 minutes.

2. In a large bowl, combine all tempura batter ingredients until a thick, but smooth consistency is reached.

3. Using your fingers, dip each piece of asparagus into the batter one at a time, shaking off excess on the inside of the bowl. Slowly lower the coated asparagus into the hot oil, careful not to splash.

Shopping List

4-6 cups **vegetable oil**, for frying
1 pound **fresh asparagus**, stalks trimmed off
TEMPURA BATTER
1 cup **soy flour**
¾ cup **club soda**
2 large **eggs**
1 tablespoon **vegetable oil**
1 tablespoon **baking powder**
⅛ teaspoon **garlic powder**
½ teaspoon **salt**
⅛ teaspoon **black pepper**

4. Fry the battered asparagus in batches of 3 pieces each, about 3 minutes or until golden brown. Let sit on paper towels to drain excess oil before serving hot.

George's Tips | Remove the asparagus stalks about 1½ inches from the bottom. The easiest way to do this is while they are all still in the grocery store's Styrofoam package or rubber banded together. You can trim the whole batch in one shot.

Variation | Make a quick dipping sauce or "aioli" for the asparagus by combining ½ cup light mayonnaise with 2 teaspoons of minced garlic, and 2 tablespoons Louisiana hot sauce. Salt to taste and serve room temperature.

Honey Mustard Chicken Skewers

calories: 275 | fat: 6.5g | protein: 48g | fiber: 0.5g | NET CARBS: **4g**

If you watch any of those travelling chef shows, I'm pretty sure that you've seen that when you combine food and sticks, you'll always get something good! Take another proven combination like honey and mustard, and you've got an appetizer that the whole family can enjoy.

Shopping List

nonstick cooking spray
2 tablespoons **brown deli mustard**
1 tablespoon **honey**
¼ teaspoon **salt**
⅛ teaspoon **onion powder**
2 pounds **boneless, skinless chicken breasts**
bamboo skewers

1. Preheat the oven to 400 degrees and spray a sheet pan with nonstick cooking spray.

2. In a large bowl, combine the brown deli mustard, honey, salt, and onion powder. Add the chicken to the bowl and toss to coat.

3. Place the coated chicken breasts on the sheet pan, and top with any remaining sauce that can be scraped from the bowl. Bake for 25 minutes, or until cutting into a breast reveals no pink, and the juices run clear.

4. Remove chicken from oven and let cool 5-10 minutes before cutting lengthwise into 1 inch strips. Thread each cooked chicken strip onto a bamboo skewer.

5. Lightly grill each skewer for about 1 minute before serving, or return to a 400 degree oven for 5 minutes to ensure that they are served hot!

George's Tips | When grilling with bamboo skewers, it is always a good idea to soak the skewers in water for 30 minutes to ensure that they don't catch on fire!

Variation | Add ¾ teaspoon of curry powder in step 2 to make Curry Honey Mustard Chicken Skewers. It's a really great combination that adds a whole lot more zing! Or skip the sticks, and skip cutting the chicken into strips, and serve the breasts whole as an entrée… though I still suggest you grill em'!

prep time	cook time	serves
10 mins	15 mins	8

Pesto Party Nuts

calories: 275 | fat: 26g | protein: 8g | fiber: 4g | NET CARBS: **3g**

We always have a bowl of mixed nuts somewhere on the table when we have guests over (as well as a ton of other food), so we're always coming up with new ways to make them interesting. These pesto flavored nuts are positively addicting and super easy to make. We save a little money by not making the pesto with the traditional pine nuts (but you can by reading the variation below), because coating nuts in nuts seemed like a little too much of a good thing!

Shopping List

1 clove **garlic**

2 tablespoons **olive oil**

⅓ cup grated **Parmesan cheese**

½ cup fresh **basil leaves**

½ teaspoon **salt**

1 cup **raw pecans**

2 cups **raw almonds**

1. Preheat oven to 350 degrees and line a sheet pan with heavy duty aluminum foil.

2. Place garlic clove, olive oil, Parmesan cheese, fresh basil, and salt in a food processor and pulse to combine. Pulse until almost entirely pureed, but still grainy.

3. Place pecans and almonds in a large mixing bowl and cover with the pureed pesto mixture. Toss all to coat well.

4. Spread the coated nuts in a single layer over the aluminum foil covered sheet pan and bake for 12-15 minutes, stirring once halfway through. Serve warm, or at room temperature.

George's Tips | Be sure to buy raw almonds and pecans in bags from the baking section of the grocery store, as the nuts sold in the snack food section are already roasted and will severely dry out, or burn, if roasted a second time!

Variation | Add a tablespoon of pine nuts to the pesto puree in step 2 for the classic pesto flavor. You can also make these with walnuts, or any raw nuts you have in your cupboard.

Sausage Stuffed Mushrooms

calories: 135 | fat: 8g | protein: 13g | fiber: 1g | NET CARBS: **4g**

These Southern style stuffed mushrooms are so good that no one would ever question their lack of breadcrumbs. The cream cheese cuts the strong flavor of the sausage and makes these so irresistible that you might just want to bake a double batch!

1. Preheat the oven to 375 degrees, and spray a baking sheet with nonstick cooking spray.

2. Wipe mushrooms clean with a damp cloth. Carefully twist stems of mushrooms off and place mushroom caps on baking sheet. Chop mushroom stems and set aside.

3. Add turkey sausage, and chopped mushroom stems to a skillet over medium-high heat and brown well. Remove from heat and drain.

4. While still hot, combine sausage and stem mixture with cream cheese, green onion, salt, and pepper to make the stuffing. Stuff each mushroom cap with a heaping spoonful of the stuffing and return to baking sheet. Bake stuffed mushrooms for 15 minutes, or until mushrooms are tender. Serve hot.

Shopping List

nonstick cooking spray

16 medium **white button mushrooms** (about **1** pound)

¼ pound **ground turkey sausage**, may use pork

2 ounces **light cream cheese**

1 green onion, thinly sliced

⅛ teaspoon **salt**

⅛ teaspoon **pepper**

George's Tips | Wiping the mushrooms clean with a damp cloth prevents the mushrooms from absorbing water and becoming too soggy, which can often happen when washing under running water. You can use turkey breakfast sausage links in this recipe; just break them up into crumbles in the browning process.

Variation | Try making these with ground Italian sausage in place of the turkey sausage (or use ground turkey Italian sausage), replacing the cream cheese with ¼ cup tomato sauce, and topping each with a pinch of grated Parmesan cheese for Italian Meat Stuffed Mushrooms!

prep time 15 mins	chill time 1 hr	serves 10

Cool Beans Salsa

calories: 200 | fat: 4.5g | protein: 12g | fiber: 10g | NET CARBS: **17g**

This simple and refreshing salsa is loaded with chickpeas (garbanzo beans) and black soy beans. Black soy beans are just like black beans, but with far less carbohydrates. Though you may have never seen them, they are usually sold in the organic section of the grocery store under the brand name Eden.

Shopping List

1 can (14-16 ounces) **chickpeas**
1 can (14-16 ounces) **black soy beans**
½ cup chopped **tomato**
⅓ cup diced **red onion**
2 tablespoons fresh chopped **cilantro**
1 tablespoon **lime juice**
salt and **pepper**

1. Drain and rinse both cans of beans, and then add to a large serving bowl.

2. Add tomato, red onion, cilantro, and lime juice to the beans and toss all to combine. Salt and pepper to taste.

3. Cover and refrigerate for at least 1 hour for the flavors to mingle. Eat as a cold bean salad, serve alongside grilled chicken skewers, or serve with whole wheat tortilla chips, if you desire.

George's Tips | Try a bowl of this beside my Southwestern Chicken Salad in Avocado Bowls, recipe page: 63, to make a full Southwestern lunch.

Variation | Add 1 teaspoon of cumin and 2 teaspoons of chili powder for a more intense flavor. ¼ cup of diced green bell pepper is also a great addition!

prep time	cook time	yield	serves
10 mins	15 mins	24 fritters	8

Ham and Cheese Fritters

calories: 260 | fat: 18g | protein: 11g | fiber: 1.5g | NET CARBS: **9g**

While party guests may not know what these are just by looking at them, once they taste them, they'll definitely be back for more. With loads of ham and sharp Cheddar cheese mixed right into the dough, they remind me of ham croquettes, only far easier to make. Just don't call them Ham and Cheese Doughnuts like I did the first time I made them (following the directions in the Variation below) or your family may be cautious to try them! Though they'll still love em' once they do!

Shopping List

4-6 cups **vegetable oil**, for frying
1 cup diced **cooked ham**
½ cup shredded **sharp Cheddar cheese**
½ cup **whole wheat flour**
¾ cup **soy flour**
3 large **eggs**
1 tablespoon **baking powder**
½ teaspoon **salt**

1. Place a pot over medium-high heat and fill with at least 3 inches of vegetable oil. Heat oil until about 350 degrees, about 5 minutes.

2. In a large bowl, combine remaining ingredients and 2 tablespoons of water, mixing well.

3. Using a teaspoon, drop walnut size amounts of the batter gently into the hot oil, careful not to splash.

4. Fry the fritters in small batches of 4 or 5 for about 3 minutes each batch or until deep golden brown. Let rest on paper towels to drain excess oil before serving hot.

George's Tips | I like to use extra sharp Cheddar cheese in these, though it takes a little more effort as they usually only sell the extra sharp in bricks that you must shred yourself. It's worth it though, as you can get a ton more flavor without having to add more cheese!

Variation | Make Monte Cristo style fritters by replacing the sharp Cheddar cheese with Swiss cheese and sprinkling the finished fritters with a small amount of bulk sugar substitute.

prep time	cook time	yield	serves
25 mins	15 mins	16 pieces	8

Devilish Eggs Au Gratin

calories: 120 | fat: 9g | protein: 9g | fiber: 0g | NET CARBS: 1g

This recipe was one of those strange ideas that just came to me one day. I thought, what would happen if I baked deviled eggs in the same way as twice baked potatoes and served them warm? The results were delicious and different; something your family or party guests will definitely remember.

1. Preheat the oven to 375 degrees and spray a baking dish with nonstick cooking spray.

2. Cut hard boiled eggs in half and transfer yolks to a small bowl.

3. Add sour cream, lemon juice, Dijon mustard, and salt, to yolks in bowl. Mash all together to make the filling.

Shopping List

nonstick cooking spray
8 hard boiled eggs, peeled
¼ cup **light sour cream**
2 teaspoons **lemon juice**
1 tablespoon **Dijon mustard**
¼ teaspoon **salt**
½ cup shredded **Swiss cheese**
2 slices **bacon**, cooked and finely crumbled

4. Fill all egg white halves with an equal amount of the yolk filling and place on baking dish, side by side, crowded close together. Cover all with the shredded Swiss cheese and bake 15 minutes, or until cheese is bubbly and melted.

5. Top with crumbled bacon pieces and serve hot.

George's Tips | These will be hot! Make sure to serve with small tongs or a cocktail fork, as most people are accustomed to reaching for the traditional (cold) deviled eggs with their fingers.

Variation | You can make these the traditional way with mayonnaise in place of the sour cream, though that will add more fat. To lower the fat, sliced green onions can be substituted for garnish in place of the crumbled bacon.

prep time	cook time	yield	serves
20 mins	10 mins	16 potstickers	8

Cabbage Wrapped Pork Pot Stickers

calories: 180 | fat: 9g | protein: 17g | fiber: 2.5g | NET CARBS: **6g**

Steamed pot stickers, or Asian dumplings, used to be one of my favorite Chinese food take-out indulgences. Traditionally wrapped in a white flour wonton skin, I've found that boiled cabbage leaves make for the perfect Good Carb reinvention of this truly great party food!

Shopping List

1 medium head **cabbage**
1 pound **lean ground pork**
2 **green onions**, chopped
2 teaspoons **sesame oil**
1 tablespoon **soy sauce**
¼ teaspoon **ground ginger**
nonstick cooking spray

1. Bring a large pot of water to a boil. Wash and cut cabbage in half. Cut the core from each half of the cabbage by slicing it out in a triangular wedge.

2. Separate at least 16 of the large outer cabbage leaves from both halves, and then add to boiling water. (Save remaining raw cabbage for coleslaw or another meal.) Boil for 2 minutes, until cabbage is crisp-tender. Use a slotted spoon to transfer cooked cabbage to a plate of paper towels to drain.

3. Prepare the pot sticker filling by combining the ground pork, chopped green onions, sesame oil, soy sauce, and ground ginger in a large mixing bowl. Use your hands to mix well.

4. Place a large nonstick pan over medium-high heat and spray with nonstick cooking spray. Form the pork filling into thick oval patties about the shape and size of your thumb.

5. Place the filling patties into the pan and cook about 4 minutes on each side, until cutting into one shows no pink throughout. Depending on the size of your pan, you may need to cook patties in 2 batches. Serve cooked pork patties alongside leaves for your guests to wrap themselves, or wrap each individually, securing with toothpicks.

George's Tips | Pot stickers are almost always served alongside a sweet and tangy dipping sauce. Make one quick with ¼ cup low-sodium soy sauce, 2 teaspoons sesame oil, 1 teaspoon minced garlic, and ½ of a packet of sugar substitute.

Variation | Though pork is more traditional, ground chicken or turkey can be substituted in its place. You can also skip wrapping the pot stickers and finely chop the cabbage raw, adding about ½ cup of it to the pork mixture. Form into balls and cook to make Asian Porcupine Meatballs.

prep time	cook time	serves
5 mins	30 mins	8

Chilly Weather Chili Chickpeas

calories: 220 | fat: 6g | protein: 10g | fiber: 10g | NET CARBS: **22g**

This crunchy snack made from wholesome chickpeas is pretty much my favorite way to eat them. Smothered in chili powder with a hint of lime—eat them by the handful, or try them in place of croutons in your next salad!

Shopping List

2 cans (14-16 ounces) **chickpeas**
2 tablespoons **olive oil**
2½ teaspoons **chili powder**
½ teaspoon **paprika**
1 teaspoon **lime juice**
¾ teaspoon **salt**

1. Preheat oven to 425 degrees and line a sheet pan with heavy duty aluminum foil. Drain and rinse chickpeas.

2. Place rinsed chickpeas in a large bowl and cover with olive oil, chili powder, paprika, lime juice, and salt. Stir all to combine and evenly coat.

3. Spread the coated chickpeas in a single layer over the aluminum foil covered sheet pan and bake for 25-30 minutes, stirring twice, until chickpeas are dark in places and crunchy on the outside. Let cool 5 minutes before serving warm.

George's Tips | These can be stored for a few days in an airtight container on the counter, though they will lose their crunchiness a few hours after making them. Baking them again for 5-10 minutes should bring some crunch back into them.

Variation | I like to sprinkle even more chili powder over the top, once the chickpeas have finished baking. I also like to add a very small pinch of cayenne pepper in step 2 for more heat.

prep time	cook time	yield	serves
15 mins	14 mins	12 skins	6

Loaded Squash Skins

calories: 130 | fat: 9g | protein: 8g | fiber: 1.5g | NET CARBS: **3.5g**

I've been making Squash Fromage (or Parmesan cheese crusted squash) for years, but it wasn't until recently that I thought of using a similar technique to recreate the classic loaded potato skin appetizer. My secret ingredient for a more potato-like flavor is the sprinkling of onion powder on the squash before loading it up with toppings.

1. Preheat the oven to 350 degrees and spray a baking sheet with nonstick cooking spray.

2. Cut ends off yellow squash, then cut each in half lengthwise. Place the halves cut side up on baking sheet.

Shopping List

nonstick cooking spray
6 small to medium **yellow squash**
salt and **pepper**
onion powder
¾ cup shredded **Cheddar cheese**
4 strips **bacon**, cooked and crumbled
⅓ cup **light sour cream**
1 **green onion**, thinly sliced

3. Sprinkle squash liberally with salt, pepper, and onion powder. Next, top each with an even amount of the Cheddar cheese and crumbled bacon.

4. Bake 12-14 minutes, or until cheese is bubbly and squash has a little bit of give to the touch. Serve garnished with a dollop of sour cream and a sprinkling of sliced green onion.

George's Tips | You can use a pointed spoon, such as a grapefruit spoon, to scoop out some of the squash's center before filling with cheese and bacon, to create something closer to a "skin". That squash is good for you though!

Variation | Substitute a light sprinkling of Italian seasoning in place of the onion powder, and a spoonful of tomato sauce, and a large pinch of mozzarella cheese in place of the other ingredients for Pizza Squash Skins!

prep time	cook time	yield	serves
30 mins	10 mins	16 tomatoes	8

Crab Meat Stuffed Cherry Tomatoes

calories: 50 | fat: 2g | protein: 4g | fiber: 0.5g | NET CARBS: **2g**

Though these bite sized appetizers take a little bit more prep work than other recipes in this book, the end result is more than worth it! Freshly cooked and flaked crab meat is best, but I'm not going to kid you on that… I buy the canned lump crab meat like everyone else! It's nearly as good and, well, as easy as opening a can!

Shopping List

1 pint **cherry tomatoes**
¾ cup **lump crab meat**, drained
2 tablespoons **light mayonnaise**
2 tablespoons **Parmesan cheese**
1 **green onion**, finely diced
1 tablespoon finely diced **red bell pepper**
⅛ teaspoon **salt**
⅛ teaspoon **black pepper**

1. Preheat the oven to 350 degrees. Take a small slice off the top and bottom of each cherry tomato, so that they will stand upright.

2. Use the small end of a melon baller, or a sharp paring knife on the top of the tomatoes to hollow them out, removing about ⅔ of the pulp, discarding.

3. In a mixing bowl, fold together remaining ingredients until well blended.

4. Stuff each hollowed out tomato until overflowing, and then place upright on a large baking sheet. Bake 7-10 minutes or just until heated through. Serve hot.

George's Tips | Though this calls for cherry tomatoes, grape tomatoes can be used if you go for the largest bunch you can find. Compari tomatoes will also work, but are far larger and will take a little longer in the oven—not to mention a knife and fork to eat!

Variation | Add ½ teaspoon of Old Bay seasoning, and a teaspoon of Dijon mustard for a little more flavor. Also, it should be mentioned that these are also quite good cold and don't require any baking at all!

| prep time 10 mins | serves 8 |

Roasted Red Pepper Spread

calories: 95 | fat: 7.5g | protein: 3.5g | fiber: 0g | NET CARBS: **4g**

Roasted red peppers make this the perfect, creamy spread for sliced raw zucchini or cucumber. Though I always keep a jar of roasted red peppers on hand, you can also make your own by grilling red bell peppers until the outer skin turns black. Let cool and peel the charred skin off. Slice off top and scoop out core before using. One large pepper will substitute for the entire jar in this recipe.

Shopping List

8 ounces **light cream cheese**
1 jar (6-8 ounces) **roasted red peppers**
⅓ cup **light sour cream**
1 clove **garlic**
5 leaves **fresh basil**
salt and **pepper**

1. Place cream cheese in a serving bowl and let soften for 15-30 minutes. Drain roasted red peppers and discard liquid.

2. Place drained red peppers, sour cream, garlic, fresh basil and a pinch of salt and pepper in a food processor or blender. Pulse the mixture until almost entirely smooth.

3. Pour blended red pepper mixture over softened cream cheese, and use a rigid spoon to fold all together. Serve immediately as a fresh vegetable spread, or chill before serving to let the flavors mingle. Garnish with fresh basil leaves, or finely diced (fresh) red bell pepper.

George's Tips | I like to swirl the blended red pepper mixture into the cream cheese only lightly, leaving a nice design and slight contrast between the two textures for serving.

Variation | Adding a teaspoon of lemon juice will give this spread a little more zing. To make more of a dip than a spread, the cream cheese can be skipped and 16 total ounces (1 regular tub) of light sour cream can be used instead.

prep time	cook time	serving	serves
10 mins	5 mins	3 pieces	8

Boneless Buffalo Wing Bites

calories: 355 | fat: 24g | protein: 30g | fiber: 0g | NET CARBS: **0g**

These bite sized indulgences are perfect for those that are really watching their carbs as they are fried (or baked!) in a coating of crushed pork rinds that really mimics the crispy skin of regular chicken wings. Of course, if pork rinds aren't your thing, you can lower the fat in this recipe significantly by simply tossing chunks of grilled chicken in the sauce.

1. Place a pot over medium-high heat and fill with at least 2 inches of vegetable oil. Heat oil 3-4 minutes, until about 350 degrees.

2. Add the pork rinds, Italian seasoning, pepper, and garlic powder to a large food storage bag and use a heavy can or similar to crush the rinds until smooth.

Shopping List

4-6 cups **vegetable oil**, for frying

1 large bag (**4** ounces) **regular pork rinds**

½ teaspoon **Italian seasoning**

¼ teaspoon **black pepper**

⅛ teaspoon **garlic powder**

1½ pounds **boneless, skinless chicken breasts**, cut in **1** inch cubes

2 large **eggs**, beaten in a bowl

¼ cup **Louisiana hot sauce**

¼ cup **trans-fat free margarine**, melted

3. Dip chicken cubes into the beaten eggs and then place into the bag of seasoned pork rinds, shaking to coat.

4. Fry the coated chicken pieces in small batches of 5 or 6 for about 3 minutes each batch, or until a deep golden brown. Let rest on paper towels to drain excess oil.

5. In a medium bowl, combine hot sauce and melted margarine to make the sauce. Toss fried and drained chicken in the sauce before serving hot. Serve garnished with celery sticks and blue cheese dressing, if desired.

George's Tips | You can lower the fat by baking them instead of frying. Simply place the coated chicken pieces on a greased sheet pan and bake at 400 degrees for about 15 minutes, or until cutting into one reveals no pink.

Variation | These are also good without a sauce at all, but if hot wing sauce isn't your thing, try topping with marinara sauce and mozzarella cheese and then broiling for just 1 minute to melt the cheese and you will have Chicken Parmesan Bites!

Honey Roasted Cashews

calories: 220 | fat: 16g | protein: 5g | fiber: 1g | NET CARBS: **12g**

Honey roasted peanuts used to be a favorite of mine before losing weight, but I know now that they are entirely (and visibly) covered in sugar. While this recipe can be made with peanuts, one day I tried recreating my old favorite with cashews and discovered that they were even better!

1. Preheat oven to 325 degrees and line a baking sheet with parchment paper.

2. In a large bowl, combine honey, vegetable oil, and water. Add cashews and toss well to coat.

Shopping List

1 tablespoon **honey**
1 tablespoon **vegetable oil**
1 tablespoon **water**
2 cups **cashews**, unsalted
2 tablespoons **bulk sugar substitute**
1 teaspoon **salt**, or less to taste

3. Spread the coated nuts in a single layer over the parchment papered baking sheet and bake for 12-15 minutes, stirring once halfway through.

4. Remove pan from oven and sprinkle cashews with sugar substitute and salt while still hot, shaking pan to evenly coat. I suggest starting with only ½ teaspoon of the salt and adding additional to taste.

George's Tips | Watch the baking cashews carefully, as you want them nice and golden brown but the honey can burn! (They'll still taste good if slightly burned and may even taste better, depending on your taste of course!)

Variation | Though it may sound strange, try adding ½ teaspoon of ground cayenne pepper for a sweet and spicy snack.

Herb Marinated Mushrooms

calories: 99 | fat: 9g | protein: 2g | fiber: 1g | NET CARBS: **2g**

These Herb Marinated Mushrooms are a really great party appetizer to make the day before a party to free up some extra prep time to make other dishes the day of. With unquestionably better taste than jarred mushrooms, and at a fraction of the cost you would pay for them by the pound at the salad bar of your local grocery store, these are a no brainer.

Shopping List

16 ounces **button mushrooms**, cleaned
¼ cup **olive oil**
2 tablespoons **red wine vinegar**
2 teaspoons **minced garlic**
1½ tablespoons fresh chopped **herbs**
½ teaspoon **salt**
⅛ teaspoon **black pepper**

1. Add all ingredients to a large food storage container with lid. Close lid and toss all to combine.

2. Refrigerate for at least 12 hours to marinate, shaking mushrooms around in the marinade once or twice to keep them evenly coated. Use a slotted spoon to transfer to a serving dish and serve chilled.

George's Tips | For the fresh herbs, I like a mixture of basil, oregano, and thyme, but you can use only oregano or only 2 of the three and they'll still be good. I also like to look through the different containers of button mushrooms at the store to find the smallest ones, as they will marinate the quickest. Larger mushrooms could take as long as 24 hours to marinate.

Variation | Make them quicker by boiling the mushrooms for 2 minutes and draining well before adding to the marinade. This way, they should be good and ready to eat in as little as 4 hours of marinating time. You can also use this boiling method to quickly marinate other vegetables like broccoli or cauliflower florets.

Breakfast and Brunch

prep time	cook time	yield	serves
5 mins	6 mins ea.	6 waffles	3

Wealth of Health Waffles

calories: 150 | fat: 9g | protein: 11g | fiber: 1.5g | NET CARBS: **6g**

These waffles are so sweet and delicious; you don't even need any syrup, though I like to mash raspberries into a syrup for mine! Though you may need to pick up a waffle iron (I would definitely suggest an electric) to make them, you can get one for under $10 these days, and it's worth it. Just try making an egg and cheese sandwich between 2 of these!

Shopping List

nonstick cooking spray
½ cup **soy flour**
¼ cup **bulk sugar substitute**
½ teaspoon **baking powder**
2 large **eggs**
⅓ cup **heavy cream**
⅓ cup **water**
1 teaspoon **vanilla extract**

1. Spray electric waffle iron with nonstick cooking spray and preheat.

2. In a large bowl, combine all ingredients until a thick, but smooth consistency is reached. If the batter is not smooth and instead, like a thick dough (which could happen, depending on the brand of soy flour), add a small amount of additional water until smooth.

3. Pour ¼ cup batter in the center of waffle iron, and close the lid. Cook for about 5 to 6 minutes, or until steam is no longer visibly coming out of the sides of the iron. Repeat until batter is used. Note: ¼ cup batter per waffle is the perfect amount for a smaller waffle iron, and should make about 6 waffles. Larger waffle irons will require ⅓ cup batter, ½ cup for a Belgian sized.

4. Serve hot, with butter, or with your favorite toppings, such as fresh fruit, whipped cream, or sugar free syrup.

George's Tips | Unsweetened soy milk can be used in place of the heavy cream in the batter, if you prefer. Do not open the waffle maker in the first 3 minutes. Some batter may escape out of the sides but that is normal until you get used to the proper amount for your maker. If you like crispy waffles like me just let them cook a minute or so longer!

Variation | These waffles are healthy enough as is, but you can add a few tablespoons of milled flax seed for added fiber! You can also add ½ teaspoon of ground cinnamon to the batter for that "cinnamon toast" experience.

prep time	cook time	serves
20 mins	35 mins	8

Blueberry Cream Cheese Crumb Cake

calories: 210 | fat: 15g | protein: 11g | fiber: 2g | NET CARBS: **7g**

This crumb cake, or Blueberry Buckle as some would call it, is by far the most stunningly complex looking baked good Rachel has ever come up with, but it's actually put together in only 20 minutes and without using any white flour or sugar!

1. Place oven rack in the center position and preheat to 375 degrees. Spray an 8 inch oven safe skillet or round cake pan with nonstick cooking spray, and sprinkle 1 tablespoon bulk sugar substitute around the bottom and edges.

2. In a large bowl, combine soy flour, ½ cup of the sugar substitute, and the baking powder. Whisk in 2 eggs, soy milk, vanilla extract, and ⅓ cup of tap water until completely mixed.

3. Fold ¼ cup of the blueberries into the batter, and then pour batter into the prepared skillet or cake pan, spreading evenly.

Shopping List

nonstick cooking spray
¾ cup **soy flour**
¾ cup + **1** tablespoon **bulk sugar substitute**
2 teaspoons **baking powder**
3 large **eggs**
½ cup **unsweetened soy milk**
1½ teaspoons **vanilla extract**
½ cup fresh **blueberries**
8 ounces **reduced fat cream cheese**, softened
3 tablespoons **trans-fat free margarine**
½ cup **almond flour**
½ teaspoon **ground cinnamon**

4. In a medium bowl, combine cream cheese and remaining 1 egg, mixing well. Pour over batter in cake pan and spread evenly. Top with remaining ¼ cup of blueberries.

5. In another bowl, combine margarine, almond flour, cinnamon, and remaining ¼ cup of sugar substitute to create the crumb topping. Crumble over top all in the cake pan.

6. Bake for 35 minutes or until a toothpick inserted into the cake comes out clean of any batter. Let cool 10 minutes before slicing into 8 equal slices.

Variation | Bake just the crumb topping of margarine, almond flour, cinnamon, and ¼ cup of sugar substitute, crumbled all over an aluminum foil lined sheet pan for 5 minutes, or until crunchy, to sprinkle over top a finished batch of Fool Proof Lemon Curd Custard, recipe page: 181.

prep time
15 mins

cook time
10 mins

serves
2

Brunch

Egg White, Spinach, and Ricotta Frittata

calories: 220 | fat: 12g | protein: 22g | fiber: 0g | NET CARBS: 4.5g

This frittata (or open faced Italian omelet) is a refreshing and light way to start your day! I've been making breakfasts like this for years as a way to use up leftover vegetables from dinner the night before. The richness of the ricotta cheese helps beef things up without nearly as much fat as the 8 egg yolks it replaces.

1. Sauté spinach in a nonstick pan over medium heat with a few tablespoons of water for 1-2 minutes, just until leaves begin to wilt. Drain well, and then pat with paper towels to soak up some of the additional moisture.

2. Place egg whites, ricotta cheese, minced garlic, salt, and pepper in a large bowl and whisk until combined and frothy.

Shopping List

2 cups **fresh spinach leaves**, packed
whites of **8** large **eggs**
⅓ cup **ricotta cheese**
2 teaspoons **minced garlic**
¼ teaspoon **salt**
⅛ teaspoon **black pepper**
1 tablespoon **olive oil**
2 tablespoons grated **Parmesan cheese**

3. Place oven rack in highest position and set oven to broil. Place olive oil and drained spinach in an oven-safe skillet on the stove over medium-high heat.

4. Pour egg white and ricotta mixture into pan and let cook until bottom begins to firm. Use a rubber spatula to gently pull up the edges and check the bottom of the frittata for doneness. Once the bottom is browned, place the entire skillet under the broiler for 1-2 minutes to cook the top of the frittata.

5. Once the top of the frittata is beginning to puff up, remove from oven and cover with Parmesan cheese. Return to the oven for an additional 30 seconds to lightly brown the Parmesan cheese before serving.

George's Tips | While I've never been a big fan of the taste of the egg "substitutes" sold in cartons, they are almost entirely comprised of egg whites and work well in this recipe. Most stores also sell cartons of 100% egg whites without the added colors and flavors.

Variation | Frozen baby broccoli florets work great in place of the spinach for a little extra texture. Garnish with a little bit of diced tomato for a splash of color.

Blue Coconut Parfaits

calories: 90 | fat: 3g | protein: 4g | fiber: 1.5g | NET CARBS: **11g**

This recipe uses a very rare type of blue coconut… just kidding! The only thing strange about this recipe is the name, as these are actually delicious blueberry and yogurt parfaits, topped with shredded (not blue!) coconut.

Shopping List

1 cup **plain low-fat yogurt**

1 tablespoon **bulk sugar substitute**

1 teaspoon fresh **lemon juice**

1 teaspoon **vanilla extract**

1½ cups **blueberries**

2 tablespoons **unsweetened shredded coconut**

1. In a bowl, whisk together the yogurt, sugar substitute, lemon juice, and vanilla.

2. Divide the blueberries among 4 wide-mouth champagne or parfait glasses and top each with equal amounts of the yogurt mixture.

3. Sprinkle each parfait with coconut and top with a single blueberry. Serve garnished with lemon, if desired!

George's Tips | Sadly, shredded coconut without any sugar added is getting harder to find in stores, but I do know that they sell it at Trader Joes. You can also make your own grated coconut from fresh coconut by using a cheese grater. Or you can skip the coconut altogether and add a drop or two of coconut extract to the yogurt in step 1.

Variation | I like to add a little crunch to these parfaits and top with coarsely chopped nuts like walnuts, pecans, almonds, peanuts, or even Rachel's favorite—sunflower seeds! Or top with my Honey Roasted Cashews, recipe page: 43. You can also make this with ricotta cheese in place of the yogurt, and if the blueberries seem a little blue, give them some company by adding in strawberry slices or even raspberries!

prep time	cook time	serves
15 mins	40 mins	8

Crustless Chicken Divan Quiche

calories: 160 | fat: 11g | protein: 14.5g | fiber: 0g | NET CARBS: **1g**

Though I must confess that I didn't make very many quiches before I started eating Stella Style, I can say that I've grown a whole new appreciation for them. What else can you throw pretty much any ingredients into and almost always end up with a good result suitable for breakfast, lunch, or dinner? When else can you eat chicken and broccoli for breakfast?

Shopping List

nonstick cooking spray
8 large **eggs**
½ cup **half and half**
½ teaspoon **salt**
⅛ teaspoon **black pepper**
⅛ teaspoon **nutmeg**
1 cup chopped **cooked chicken**
1 cup **frozen broccoli florets**
1 cup shredded **sharp Cheddar cheese**

1. Preheat the oven to 350 degrees and spray a 9 inch baking dish or pie pan with nonstick cooking spray.

2. Mix the eggs, half and half, salt, pepper, and nutmeg in a bowl, and then pour the mixture into the baking dish.

3. Sprinkle the chicken, broccoli florets, and Cheddar cheese over the top, and then push them down into the egg mixture with your hands or the back of a spoon, until all are mostly submerged.

4. Bake for about 40 minutes, until the top of the quiche turns golden brown and a toothpick inserted into the center comes out clean. Let rest for 5 minutes to set before slicing.

George's Tips | A hearty quiche like this one can make a great dinner too! It's just light enough to leave room for dessert! Oh, and don't forget a mixed salad to start.

Variation | Make a Chicken Florentine Quiche by substituting ⅔ of a cup of cooked and drained spinach in place of the broccoli, and ½ cup of grated Parmesan cheese in place of the Cheddar.

prep time	cook time	yield	serves
15 mins	25 mins	6 muffins	6

Sweet Potato Muffins

calories: 205 | fat: 14g | protein: 9g | fiber: 4g | NET CARBS: **9g**

These Southern muffins make a great side dish for any breakfast or brunch, as they are a little more savory than the typical muffin (even though they're named for being "sweet"). Without a doubt, they are best served smeared with butter or cream cheese.

Shopping List

nonstick cooking spray

1½ cups **almond flour**

1 cup cooked **sweet potato**, roughly mashed

3 large **eggs**

½ cup **bulk sugar substitute**

1 teaspoon **vanilla extract**

1 teaspoon **baking powder**

1 teaspoon **ground cinnamon**

¼ teaspoon **nutmeg**

1. Place the baking rack in the center of the oven and preheat the oven to 375 degrees. Spray a 6 cup muffin pan with nonstick cooking spray, or use a silicone muffin pan for even better results. (We photographed the muffins in paper liners, but have since found that we have better results without liners.)

2. Mix all of the ingredients in a bowl with a wooden spoon until well blended. Fill the muffin cups with the batter evenly until all has been used.

3. Bake for 25 minutes, until the muffin tops turn golden brown and a toothpick stuck into the center comes out clean.

4. Remove the muffins from the oven and let cool for 5 minutes before serving warm or at room temperature.

George's Tips | The quickest way to make the mashed sweet potato for this recipe is to puncture 1 large sweet potato with a fork and microwave on a plate for 4-5 minutes, flipping once. Let cool, then slice in half, and use a spoon to scoop out the meat to measure out 1 cup. Lightly mash.

Variation | I like to add ¼ cup chopped pecans to the batter to add a little more texture.

Plant City Strawberry Spinach Salad

Plant City Strawberry Spinach Salad

calories: 85 | fat: 7g | protein: 1.5g | fiber: 2g | NET CARBS: **3.5g**

I'm lucky enough to live only a few miles from Plant City, Florida, the "Winter Strawberry Capital of the World", so I can get the freshest strawberries for this decidedly summery brunch-time salad smack dab in the dead of winter! Of course, the other thing about living in Florida is that I also get the summer heat in the middle of winter to need such a refreshing salad that time of year in the first place!

Shopping List

VINAIGRETTE

1 tablespoon **balsamic vinegar**
6 hulled **strawberries**
¼ teaspoon **salt**
⅛ teaspoon **black pepper**
2 tablespoons **olive oil**

SALAD

6 ounces **fresh spinach leaves**
thinly sliced **red onion**
½ cup hulled and sliced **strawberries**

1. Create the dressing by adding balsamic vinegar, 6 hulled strawberries, salt, and pepper to a food processor or blender. Blend until strawberries are pureed. If you can't get them to puree all the way, simply add a tablespoon of water to loosen things up.

2. While blending, slowly drizzle the 2 tablespoons of olive oil into the dressing to create an emulsified vinaigrette. Transfer to a serving carafe or dish.

3. Prepare the salad by piling an equal amount of spinach leaves across 4 bowls. Top each salad with a few thin slices of red onion (to your liking) and ¼ of the sliced strawberries. Serve drizzled with the vinaigrette.

George's Tips | If bitter, you may want to add as much as 1 tablespoon of bulk sugar substitute or honey to the dressing to taste, depending on how ripe your strawberries are and how sweet your balsamic vinegar is.

Variation | This basic salad can be modified in innumerable ways, depending on your tastes. You can add strips of grilled chicken, toasted walnuts (bake raw, shelled walnuts at 350 degrees for 5-10 minutes until aromatic), gorgonzola cheese, or some combination of all three. A pinch of poppy seeds in the dressing is also a nice touch.

| Zucchini Crusted Quiche

prep time	cook time	serves
15 mins	40 mins	8

Zucchini Crusted Quiche

calories: 150 | fat: 10g | protein: 12g | fiber: 0.5g | NET CARBS: **3g**

The fact that this Italian inspired quiche doesn't start with a pie crust doesn't mean it doesn't have a crust at all! Did you get all that? What I meant was… zucchini is delicious! This description is proof positive that there are stranger things in the world than a zucchini crusted quiche.

1. Preheat the oven to 350 degrees and spray an 9 inch baking dish or pie pan with nonstick cooking spray.

2. Cut ends off zucchini and discard. Thinly slice zucchini on a bias or into discs, and lay them evenly across the bottom of the baking dish. Start with the bottom, and then line the edges of the baking dish. Once finished, sprinkle the oregano over top.

Shopping List

nonstick cooking spray
2 medium **zucchini**
¼ teaspoon **dry oregano**
6 large **eggs**
½ cup **half and half**
½ teaspoon **salt**
⅛ teaspoon **black pepper**
⅛ teaspoon **garlic powder**
1½ cups shredded **mozzarella cheese**
¼ cup **Parmesan cheese**

3. Mix the eggs, heavy cream, salt, pepper, garlic powder, and mozzarella cheese in a bowl, and then pour the mixture over the zucchini in the baking dish.

4. Sprinkle the Parmesan cheese over the top, and then push it down into the egg mixture with your hands or the back of a spoon, until mostly submerged.

5. Bake for about 40 minutes, until the top of the quiche turns golden brown and a toothpick inserted into the center comes out clean. Let rest for 5 minutes to set before slicing.

George's Tips | If you have more than enough zucchini to line the bottom of the dish, chop the extra up and add it into the quiche in step 4. Or arrange some of the zucchini discs on the quiche's top for a nicer presentation.

Variation | Go even more Italian by browning pancetta (Italian bacon) in a skillet over medium-high heat, draining well, and adding it to the quiche in step 4.

| prep time 10 mins | cook time 14 mins | serves 6 |

Cheesy Ham and Egg Quick Cups

calories: 190 | fat: 13g | protein: 15.5g | fiber: 0g | NET CARBS: **1.5g**

Making breakfast in a muffin pan is an impressive, and time saving tip when cooking for a crowd. You could even double this recipe, prepping everything in the pans the night before, and simply pop it in the oven the next morning. In 14 minutes, you've got breakfast for 12!

1. Place the rack in the center position, and preheat the oven to 375 degrees. Spray a 6 cup muffin pan, or silicone muffin pan, with nonstick cooking spray.

Shopping List

nonstick cooking spray
6 slices (**1** ounce each) **ham**
6 large **eggs**
⅛ teaspoon **salt**
⅛ teaspoon **black pepper**
1 cup shredded **Cheddar cheese**

2. Line each of the muffin cups with a slice of ham. Fold the ham slices if too large so the ends stick up above the top of the tin.

3. Whisk the eggs together with the salt and pepper, and pour equally into each of the 6 ham lined muffin cups.

4. Top each with an even amount of the Cheddar cheese and bake 12-14 minutes, or until cheese is bubbly and eggs are slightly firm. Let stand for 2 minutes, then remove from pan, and serve garnished with a sprinkling of sliced green onion or chives if desired.

George's Tips | Egg whites or Eggbeaters may be used in place of whole eggs to lower cholesterol in this recipe. Try halving the amount of cheese or using low-fat cheese to go even healthier still!

Variation | There are almost limitless combinations of great breakfasts you can make as simply as this one! To make a Mexican version: use cooked Chorizo in place of the ham and top with salsa. To make an Italian version: replace the ham with pepperoni, and replace the Cheddar with mozzarella cheese; garnish with fresh basil.

Lunchtime Favorites

Southwestern Chicken Salad in Avocado Bowls

calories: 395 | fat: 15g | protein: 55g | fiber: 3g | NET CARBS: **3g**

You know, I'd never written a chicken salad recipe before this book, as I just didn't know if I had one interesting enough. Well I can tell you that THIS one is interesting! Not only is it sour cream and salsa based, rather than mayonnaise based, but it's served right in half of an avocado. Just make sure to scoop the avocado out with a fork as you eat it!

Shopping List

2 cups **cooked chicken**, shredded
⅔ cup **light sour cream**
3 tablespoons **chunky salsa**
1 tablespoon fresh chopped **cilantro**
1 teaspoon **lime juice**
2 **avocadoes**

1. Fold chicken, sour cream, salsa, cilantro, and lime juice together in a large bowl, shredding chicken with a fork until your desired consistency is reached.

2. Cover and refrigerate chicken salad for 30 minutes for the ingredients and flavors to mingle, or skip to the next step to serve immediately.

3. When you are ready to serve, slice the avocadoes in half lengthwise and remove the pit. Use each half as a serving bowl for 1 person, stuffing chicken salad into the empty pit cavity and then mounding heaping spoonfuls over top of the entire surface of the avocado half. Serve garnished with fresh cilantro.

George's Tips | When shopping, look for a chunky salsa without any added sugar or corn syrup in the ingredients list. I've found that Pace's Chunky Salsa does not add sugar and they should be readily available in any grocery store.

Variation | Give the salad more texture by adding 2 tablespoons of diced green bell pepper or a few teaspoons of diced jalapeño pepper, if you like spice. You can also serve topped with shredded Cheddar jack cheese and chopped bacon for even more great flavors!

Creamy Tomato Soup

calories: 95 | fat: 6g | protein: 3.5g | fiber: 1.5g | NET CARBS: **5g**

Canned cream of tomato soup is a classic in any family, but it almost always has high fructose corn syrup in the ingredients! My version is homemade in mere minutes and includes fresh diced tomatoes to add a little texture. (The chunks of tomato also prove that it's homemade. You made it, so take the credit!)

Shopping List

2 medium **tomatoes**, diced
1 can (**8 ounces**) **tomato sauce**
1¼ cups **vegetable broth**
½ cup **heavy cream**
1 tablespoon **tomato paste**
1½ teaspoons **bulk sugar substitute**
salt

1. Add diced tomatoes, tomato sauce, vegetable broth, heavy cream, tomato paste, and bulk sugar substitute to a pot over medium-high heat.

2. Bring up to a simmer, stirring periodically. Simmer for 10 minutes, salt to taste, and serve hot. Garnish with fresh basil or grated Parmesan cheese, if desired.

George's Tips | The tomato sauce in this recipe refers to the small cans of pure tomato sauce, sold near the tomato paste—not jarred pasta sauce. For a lower fat soup, simply replace the heavy cream with unsweetened soy milk.

Variation | You can make this recipe easier (but not fresher!) by substituting 1 (14-16 ounce) can of diced tomatoes, with their liquid for the 2 tomatoes in the shopping list. I like to add a pinch of fresh, chopped basil to the soup before simmering, but that may not be a hit with the kids!

Philly Steak Salad

calories: 375 | fat: 20g | protein: 43g | fiber: 1g | NET CARBS: **3g**

Philly Steak Sandwiches are as common as apple pie and almost as popular… they're a true American comfort food! I travel to Philadelphia frequently where you can find Philly steak sandwiches on every corner, but since I don't eat giant white flour hoagie buns, when I go out to eat I ask for mine over a house salad and they usually give it to me at no extra charge. Now if you ordered a steak salad at a fine restaurant it would cost a bundle!

1. Heat the oil in a large skillet over medium-high heat.

2. Add the peppers, steak, salt, garlic powder, and black pepper to the skillet and cook for about 5 minutes, or until the peppers are tender. Turn off heat.

Shopping List

2 tablespoons **canola oil**

1 cup fresh or frozen **red and green bell pepper** strips

16 ounces **leftover steak**, shredded or thinly sliced

⅓ teaspoon **salt**

¼ teaspoon **garlic powder**

⅛ teaspoon **black pepper**

1 cup shredded **mozzarella cheese**

4 cups any **mixed salad greens** or shredded **iceberg lettuce**

3. Top the hot steak and peppers with the cheese and let melt.

4. Divide the salad mix between 4 plates or bowls, and top each with an even amount of the hot mixture. Serve immediately.

George's Tips | A favorite place of mine in Philly makes this salad especially for me when I am in town, except they use Gruyere cheese and it is delicious. Try it! If you don't have any leftovers, you can also make these using frozen minute steaks like Steak-Ums.

Variation | In Philly they don't stop at beef—try making this same exact recipe using chicken, shrimp, tuna, crab, or just about any protein you can think of—after all, everything goes better with cheese!

| Herb Roasted Butternut Squash Soup

prep time	cook time	serves
20 mins	55 mins	6

Herb Roasted Butternut Squash Soup

calories: 150 | fat: 3.5g | protein: 6g | fiber: 5g | NET CARBS: 23g

I am almost certain that this hearty soup would hit the spot on a cold winter day. Too bad I first made it after I moved from Connecticut down to Florida, so I haven't had a chance to test that theory out yet! I've got it on my to-do list for this winter's 2 days of Florida chill!

1. Preheat the oven to 400 degrees. Slice the butternut squash in half lengthwise, and use a pointed spoon to remove seeds.

2. Coat the bottom of a sheet pan in the olive oil, and place the garlic cloves, sage leaves, and thyme on it in two equal piles. Place each half of the squash over each pile, to infuse with their flavor while roasting. Bake for 40-45 minutes, or until squash is fork tender. Remove from oven and let cool.

Shopping List

2 ⅓ – 3 pound **butternut squash**
1 tablespoon **olive oil**
4 cloves **garlic**
10 leaves **sage**
2 sprigs **thyme**
3 cups **chicken broth**
1 cup **unsweetened soy milk**
salt
sour cream, optional

3. Once the squash is cooled, use a spoon to scoop the flesh from the skin, transferring to a blender or food processor. Squeeze baked garlic cloves out of their peel and into blender with squash. Discard baked herbs. Blend squash in 2 or 3 batches, thinning it out with as much of the 3 cups chicken broth as you need to get it to blend smooth.

4. Transfer blended batches of squash to a pot over medium-high heat, and add remaining chicken stock, and soy milk. Bring up to a simmer, salt to taste, and serve hot. Garnish with a dollop of sour cream, if desired.

George's Tips | Prepare the roasted and blended squash the night before and you can heat lunch up on the stove in minutes!

Variation | Make this into a cold dessert soup by replacing the olive oil with butter; skipping the garlic, herbs, and chicken broth. Blend the squash in batches with 2 cups water, and 2 cups unsweetened soy milk. Season with a dash of cinnamon, and a dash of nutmeg. Add sugar substitute to taste, chill, and serve topped with fresh whipped cream!

Green Bean, Tomato, and Salami Salad with Tangy Italian Dressing

calories: 145 | fat: 12g | protein: 4g | fiber: 2g | NET CARBS: **4g**

This easy dish reminds me of an Italian pasta salad, with crunchy green beans in place of the pasta. Starting with frozen green beans saves a ton of snapping and steaming time with almost indistinguishable results from fresh. Frozen vegetables have come a long way—we even used them in the photograph!

1. Let green beans thaw on counter for 45 minutes before preparing. Slice salami into ¼ inch thick matchsticks about 1½ inches long.

2. Slice tops off of tomatoes and then slice each into 8 wedges.

3. Create the dressing by adding the Dijon mustard, white wine vinegar and Italian seasoning to a large mixing bowl. Whisk rapidly as you slowly pour in the olive oil until all is combined and creamy. Add salt and pepper to taste, though I suggest about ⅛ a teaspoon of each.

Shopping List

SALAD

6 ounces thick cut **salami**

1 bag (14-16 ounces) **frozen whole green beans**

3 medium **tomatoes**

3 tablespoons finely diced **red onion**

TANGY ITALIAN DRESSING

2 teaspoons **Dijon mustard**

2 tablespoons **white wine vinegar**

½ teaspoon **Italian seasoning**

¼ cup **olive oil**

salt and **pepper** to taste

4. Add thawed green beans, sliced salami, tomato wedges, and diced red onion to the large mixing bowl containing the dressing and toss all to coat. Cover and refrigerate for 1-2 hours to marinate before serving.

George's Tips | You can make this even easier with about ½ cup of store bought Italian dressing; just make sure to read the ingredients for added sugar as some Italian dressings can have as much as 8 grams of the stuff per serving!

Variation | Adding 4 slices of provolone cheese, sliced into thin strips, takes this salad to an even greater place!

Cucumber Dill Salad

calories: 105 | fat: 7g | protein: 3g | fiber: 1g | NET CARBS: **7g**

This refreshing salad is the perfect side dish for an afternoon grilling, and proof that cucumber is more than just a garnish. It falls somewhere in between a Greek Tzatziki sauce and a chunky dill potato salad... without all the starch. It's cool, delicious and good not just with grilled meat, but ON it! With sour cream and a tinge of sweet from apple cider vinegar, the cucumber still shines through and finally gets its starring role.

Shopping List

2 medium **cucumbers**

1 cup **reduced fat sour cream**

2 tablespoons finely diced **yellow onion**

2 teaspoons fresh chopped **dill**

1 tablespoon **cider vinegar**

salt and **pepper**

1. Peel cucumbers. Slice off ends and discard. Slice in half lengthwise, and then slice the halves into thin half moons.

2. Combine reduced fat sour cream, diced yellow onion, chopped dill, and cider vinegar in a large bowl, stirring well. Add cucumbers to the mixture and toss all to coat. Salt and pepper to taste.

3. Refrigerate for at least 30 minutes (the longer, the better) before serving ice cold, garnished with fresh dill.

George's Tips | When peeling the cucumbers, I like to leave about ⅓ of the cucumber's peel intact for texture. Simply use a peeler down the length of the cucumber, skipping a strip every inch or so.

Variation | White vinegar or even lemon juice can be used in place of the cider vinegar, if that is all you have on hand. Plain yogurt or Greek yogurt (even better!) can be used in place of the sour cream. Try replacing the dill with fresh mint for something completely different, but great!

Qunch

Skillet Turkey Tetrazzini

calories: 300 | fat: 16g | protein: 28g | fiber: 0g | NET CARBS: **5g**

This no-bake recipe for creamy Tetrazzini style turkey is an easily thrown together lunch for the day after leftovers of a turkey dinner. Of course, I've also included a variation at the bottom of the page for making it as a more traditional, baked casserole.

1. Add the margarine, mushrooms, and onions to a large skillet over medium-high heat and cook for 2 minutes, just until almost tender.

2. Add the cooked turkey and sauté for just 1 more minute to warm it up before covering with the soy milk.

3. Bring the soy milk to a simmer before stirring in the cream cheese, chicken base, and pepper until smooth.

Shopping List

2 tablespoons **trans-fat free margarine**

8 ounces sliced **mushrooms**

¼ cup diced **yellow onion**

2½ cups **cooked turkey**, large chopped

1 cup **unsweetened soy milk**

8 ounces **reduced fat cream cheese**, softened

1 teaspoon **chicken base**

¼ teaspoon ground **black pepper**

1 cup shredded **Swiss cheese**

4. Add the Swiss cheese, stirring constantly until melted. Immediately remove the skillet from the heat and serve over cooked spaghetti squash, steamed cauliflower or broccoli, or whole wheat noodles.

George's Tips | I always add 2 ounces of cream sherry to Turkey Tetrazzini, though I realize that most people don't keep it in their kitchen. Grab a bottle of it in the wine department of your grocery store and add in between steps 2 and 3, the alcohol cooks out and it is good!

Variation | Make as a traditional casserole by adding 2 cups of cooked spaghetti squash or steamed cauliflower to a 2½ quart baking dish and covering with the cooked turkey. Prepare the rest of the dish as written, disregarding the turkey, and then pour the finished sauce over all in the baking dish. Make a crunchy topping by sprinkling with ¼ cup of almond flour and ¼ cup of Parmesan cheese, and then bake at 375 degrees for 20-25 minutes or until the top begins to brown.

Southern Dill Pickle Chicken Salad

calories: 175 | fat: 8.5g | protein: 21g | fiber: 0g | NET CARBS: **2.5g**

We love to make chicken salad out of leftover roast chicken, especially the pre-cooked grocery store rotisserie chickens we'll pick up in a pinch on a busy day. Rachel usually makes her own sweet relish out of cucumbers from her garden, but one day when there was no sweet relish in the fridge, I whipped up a batch of this delicious Southern Dill Pickle Chicken Salad from a jar of crunchy dills in the fridge.

Shopping List

2 cups **cooked chicken**, shredded
¼ cup finely diced **dill pickle**
1 **hardboiled egg**, peeled and diced
⅔ cup **light mayonnaise**
⅛ teaspoon **onion powder**
¼ teaspoon **black pepper**
½ packet **sugar substitute**, optional

1. Fold all ingredients together in a large bowl, shredding chicken with a fork until it is at your desired consistency. The sugar substitute is optional, but adds a nice balance to the salty dill pickles.

2. Cover and refrigerate for 30 minutes for the ingredients and flavors to mingle, or serve immediately. Serve over a green salad or alongside one of my Bran Muffins, recipe page: 176. Garnish with fresh dill if you have any on hand.

George's Tips | I like to finely mince ⅓ of the chicken in a food processor and shred the remaining ⅔ with a fork to make a salad that is the best of both worlds; ground and chunky.

Variation | Make an entirely different Dill Chicken Salad by replacing the dill pickle with fresh cucumber, and adding ¼ teaspoon of salt, and 2 teaspoons of chopped fresh dill.

Thai Chicken Lettuce Wraps

calories: 153 | fat: 7g | protein: 19g | fiber: 1g | NET CARBS: **2g**

Lettuce wraps have been a low carb staple for some time now, but have only recently taken off in popular Asian restaurants as a really great appetizer or lunch dish for everyone, regardless of whether they're watching their carbs! You see, I've been saying it for years now—naturally low carb and good carb foods are just plain good!

Shopping List

2 tablespoons **canola oil**
1 pound **chicken breast**, sliced
½ cup sliced **snow peas** (may use frozen)
½ cup shredded **carrots**
2 tablespoons sliced **green onion**
2 tablespoons **low-sodium soy sauce**
1 tablespoon **natural peanut butter**
6 large **lettuce leaves**, iceberg or Romaine

1. Heat the oil in a large skillet over medium-high heat.

2. Add the chicken, snow peas , carrots, and onions and cook for about 4 minutes, or until the chicken is cooked and the vegetables are tender.

3. Stir in the soy sauce and peanut butter, and cook for just 1 minute more. Remove from heat.

4. Divide the mixture between the 6 lettuce leaves, roll up and secure with a toothpick to serve.

George's Tips | I like to add ¼ teaspoon of crushed red pepper to the stir fry to make a spicy wrap!

Variation | Making wraps is a great way to utilize leftover meat, rather than starting from raw chicken. Try thinly slicing leftover steak or grilled chicken and adding to the skillet in step 3.

Instant Insalata Caprese

calories: **160** | fat: **12g** | protein: **10g** | fiber: **1g** | NET CARBS: **2g**

Insalata Caprese or Caprese Salads are about as Italian as it gets—with tomato, mozzarella, and basil—you've got not only the classic flavors of Italy, but the colors of their flag! Traditionally arranged on a serving platter in neat little stacks (see variation below), this recipe forgoes those time consuming arrangements for a party sized bowl that you can simply throw together.

Shopping List

1 pint **cherry tomatoes**, halved
1 pint fresh **mini mozzarella**, drained
2 tablespoons **olive oil**
1 tablespoon **balsamic vinegar**
10 fresh **basil leaves**
salt and **pepper**

1. Combine cherry tomatoes, fresh mozzarella, olive oil, and balsamic vinegar in a large serving bowl.

2. Tear basil into smaller pieces with your fingers and add to the bowl, tossing all to combine.

3. Add pinches of salt and pepper to taste. Kosher salt is best, as is freshly ground black pepper. Chill for at least 30 minutes to let the flavors mingle before serving.

George's Tips | The fresh mini mozzarella listed in the shopping list refers to clear plastic tubs of small mozzarella balls floating in water, usually sold in the fine cheese section of the grocery store's deli. The mozzarella usually comes in several different sizes, ranging from the size of a pea on up. If the only fresh mozzarella they have is too large for a single bite, you may want to halve or slice before adding to the salad.

Variation | Make a traditional Caprese Salad by buying large Roma tomatoes and a large ball of fresh mozzarella. Slice both the tomatoes and mozzarella into thick slices. Stack 1 slice of mozzarella on top of each slice of tomato, and then top with 1 large basil leaf. Drizzle olive oil and balsamic over all stacks, and then sprinkle with salt and pepper.

Lunch

prep time	chill time	serves
20 mins	1 hr	8

Cool Cauliflower and Pecan Salad

calories: 130 | fat: 11g | protein: 2.5g | fiber: 3g | NET CARBS: **4g**

Lunch

This simple cold salad is a great take-along dish for parties or get-togethers. Tangy and somewhat sweet, it's a refreshing change from the usual potato and macaroni salads that people sometimes bring, not to mention WAY lower in carbohydrates!

Shopping List

1 medium head **cauliflower**
1 cup **light mayonnaise**
2 tablespoons **cider vinegar**
¼ cup diced **yellow onion**
1½ tablespoons **bulk sugar substitute**
¾ cup **pecan halves**

1. Bring a large pot of water to a boil over high heat.

2. Clean and cut cauliflower into small florets. Cook florets in boiling water for 2-4 minutes, or until only slightly tender.

3. Drain well. Carefully pat the cooked cauliflower dry between several layers of paper towels and then add to a large serving bowl.

4. Add all remaining ingredients to the cauliflower and toss until mayonnaise is dispersed and everything is evenly coated.

5. Chill for at least 1 hour to let the flavors mingle before serving.

George's Tips | You'll definitely want a slight crunch to the cauliflower, so be careful not to overcook. You're looking for just a little bit of softness on the outside.

Variation | Add ½ cup of chopped apple, ¼ cup of diced celery, and a pinch of nutmeg to make a Cauliflower Waldorf Salad!

Poultry

Mushroom Swiss Smothered Chicken Breasts shown with Roasted Brussels Sprouts, page 143

Mushroom Swiss Smothered Chicken Breasts

calories: 405 | fat: 15g | protein: 63g | fiber: 0.5g | NET CARBS: **3g**

This is a simple recipe based on a way that I cook chicken all the time, smothered in mushrooms and cheese (and sometimes bacon—see Variation below). As a chef, I can take recipes like this for granted, as I usually don't think they're elaborate enough for a recipe... but then I remember, this is exactly how us chefs eat on our days off, so why wouldn't everyone want to cook like this on their days off?

Shopping List

2 tablespoons **trans-fat free margarine**
4 boneless, skinless chicken breasts
salt and **pepper**
8 ounces **mushrooms**, sliced
¼ teaspoon **garlic powder**
4 slices **Swiss cheese**

1. Add the margarine to a large skillet over medium-high to high heat. Once sizzling, add chicken breasts and sprinkle liberally with salt and pepper.

2. Cook chicken until golden brown, about 3-4 minutes per side.

3. Add mushrooms over chicken and sprinkle garlic powder, as well as another small pinch of salt and pepper over top. Cover, reduce heat to low, and cook an additional 5 minutes, or until cutting into chicken at its thickest part reveals no pink.

4. Place oven rack about 6 inches from the top, set broiler to high and transfer chicken breasts to a sheet pan. Top chicken breasts with an even amount of the cooked mushrooms, and then cover all with the juices from the pan. Then top each with a slice of Swiss cheese.

5. Broil for only 1 to 2 minutes or until cheese is bubbly and melted. Serve immediately.

George's Tips | Mushrooms can be purchased pre-sliced to save time, though I find that slicing them myself is faster as pre-sliced mushrooms are a pain to wash!

Variation | A slice of ham or two strips of bacon can be added between the mushrooms and the Swiss cheese for even more smothered goodness!

Cilantro Lime Chicken Thighs

calories: 290 | fat: 11g | protein: 44g | fiber: 0g | NET CARBS: 0.5g

Other than my secret ingredient of soy sauce, these chicken thighs are marinated in a typical fajita marinade. So why not make them into a full fajita platter with my Cool Beans Salsa, recipe page: 30, Southwestern Cauliflower Mash, recipe page: 146, fresh avocado, and a dollop of sour cream?

Shopping List

2 pounds **boneless, skinless chicken thighs**
2 tablespoons fresh chopped **cilantro**
juice of **1 lime**
1 tablespoon **soy sauce**
1 teaspoon **minced garlic**
2 teaspoons **bulk sugar substitute**, optional

1. In a large food storage bag or container, combine the chicken thighs, cilantro, lime juice, soy sauce, garlic, and sugar substitute. Seal or close the container and shake to coat.

2. Refrigerate for at least 1 hour to marinate. Bake or grill to serve, garnished with fresh cilantro leaves.

Baking | Preheat the oven to 400 degrees and spray a sheet pan with nonstick cooking spray. Place the marinated chicken thighs on the sheet pan, and bake for 25-30 minutes, or until cutting into a thigh reveals that it is fully cooked through.

Grilling | Grill over medium heat or slightly off of the direct fire for about 6 minutes on each side for small thighs. 7-8 minutes on each side for larger thighs, even more if using bone-in! Chicken thighs char easily, so if that isn't your thing, I'd recommend pre-baking according to directions above and only "kissing" on the grill for about 1 minute on each side.

George's Tips | You can also make this just as easily with boneless, skinless chicken breasts if you prefer.

Variation | Turn this into Spicy Chipotle Lime Chicken Thighs by adding a tablespoon of the sauce from a can of "chipotle chilies in adobo sauce", found in the Mexican foods aisle, to the marinade in step 1.

Almond Pesto Chicken

calories: 490 | fat: 27g | protein: 58g | fiber: 1g | NET CARBS: **1g**

Pesto is usually one of those love it or hate it kind of flavors (like curry), and it's usually the pine nuts to blame. I love the strong flavor of pine nuts, but I can't deny that they are getting to be a little pricey. This pesto topped chicken replaces the pine nuts with the mild, nutty taste of almonds... they're not only cheaper, but just so happen to be lower in fat and higher in fiber.

Shopping List

⅓ cup + 2 teaspoons **olive oil**
¼ cup **slivered almonds**
1 clove **garlic**
1 cup **basil leaves**, packed
¼ cup grated **Parmesan cheese**
4 boneless, skinless chicken breasts
salt and **pepper**

1. Preheat the oven to 375 degrees and grease a sheet pan with the 2 teaspoons of olive oil. (Or spray with nonstick cooking spray.)

2. Place remaining ⅓ cup olive oil, slivered almonds, garlic clove, basil leaves, and Parmesan cheese in a food processor and pulse to combine. Pulse until almost entirely pureed, but still grainy.

3. Place chicken breasts on greased sheet pan and sprinkle liberally with salt and pepper. Top each breast with an equal amount of the pesto puree, spreading to cover evenly.

4. Bake for 25-30 minutes, or until chicken is thoroughly cooked throughout. Serve garnished with fresh basil.

George's Tips | Slivered almonds are usually sold in the baking aisle and work best as they are blanched white, and will not turn the beautiful green pesto brown.

Variation | Top with thick cut, fresh tomato slices before baking for more flavor and color. Also, you could always make this the traditional way, with pine nuts in place of the almonds. Or go half and half for the flavor of traditional pesto with less fat.

Spinach and Feta Chicken Breast Roulades

Spinach and Feta Chicken Breast Roulades

calories: 355 | fat: 12g | protein: 56g | fiber: 1g | NET CARBS: **0.5**

Chefs love rolling foods into nice little packages. I think we do it just to prove that we can, though it also keeps dinner interesting! While I'll admit that this is probably the most prep intensive recipe in the book, I've included easier instructions for an "unrolled" version at the bottom of the page.

1. Preheat the oven to 400 degrees and grease a sheet pan with the 2 tablespoons of olive oil.

2. Pound the chicken breasts until about ⅓ inch thick at all parts. The easiest and cleanest way to do this is to place them into a food storage bag one at a time, close the bag and (carefully!) pound with a mallet, heavy rolling pin, or large can from the pantry.

Shopping List

2 tablespoons **olive oil**

4 boneless, skinless chicken breasts

¾ teaspoon **salt**

¼ teaspoon **black pepper**

½ teaspoon **Italian seasoning**

2 teaspoons **minced garlic**

⅓ cup **feta cheese crumbles**

1¼ cups thawed and drained, **frozen chopped spinach**

3. Place pounded chicken breasts on oiled sheet pan and cover with salt, pepper, and Italian seasoning. Flip chicken breasts in the oil on the pan to coat well and disperse the seasonings to both sides.

4. In a mixing bowl, combine minced garlic, feta cheese, and thawed and drained spinach. Spoon an equal amount of the spinach and feta filling down each chicken breast lengthwise, packing it in a neat row for easier rolling. Roll the sides of the chicken breasts up and over the filling, until overlapping.

5. Flip breasts, so that the overlapping ends are down, and bake 20 minutes, or until chicken is thoroughly cooked through and slicing into one reveals no pink.

George's Tips | For great party appetizers: simply slice the roulades into thin pinwheels and arrange on a large platter!

Variation | Follow the recipe, but make this easier and "unrolled" by skipping the pounding process and baking the chicken breasts whole for 20 minutes. Then top each breast with ¼ of the spinach mixture and return to the oven for an additional 5 minutes or until cooked through.

Lemon Caper Chicken

calories: 205 | fat: 8g | protein: 30g | fiber: 0g | NET CARBS: **1g**

Once you've got this simple recipe for sautéed chicken with lemon and capers down, the possibilities are endless. Just read the variations at the bottom of the page to see how you can change out one ingredient to make Chicken Francais, or one ingredient to make Chicken Piccata. This is classic French cooking, just minus the white flour and full fat butter, and I promise you won't miss either!

Shopping List

2 eggs, beaten
salt and **pepper**
1 pound **chicken breast cutlets**
2 tablespoons **trans-fat free margarine**
juice of **1 lemon**
⅓ cup **chicken broth**
1 tablespoon finely chopped **red onion**
1½ tablespoons **capers**, drained

1. In a large bowl, season the beaten eggs well with pinches of salt and pepper. Place the chicken cutlets in the bowl and toss to coat.

2. Add 1 tablespoon of the trans-fat free margarine to a large nonstick pan over medium-high to high heat until almost smoking hot.

3. Add in the egg coated chicken cutlets to the pan one at a time. Cook for 2-3 minutes, until bottom is golden brown, and then flip.

4. Add the lemon juice, chicken broth, and onions and continue to cook for 3 minutes more, or until the chicken is thoroughly cooked.

5. Remove from heat and stir in capers and remaining tablespoon of margarine, until sauce is creamy. Serve immediately. Garnish with fresh lemon wedges and parsley.

George's Tips | I like to rinse jarred capers before adding them to the dish right before serving, as the brine in the jar can overpower the flavor of the sauce.

Variation | Add a teaspoon of minced garlic for even more flavor. Skip the capers and replace the chicken stock with wine to make Chicken Francais. Keep the capers and add the wine, and you've got Piccata.

Easy Oregano Marinated Chicken Breasts

calories: 295 | **fat: 6g** | **protein: 54g** | **fiber: 0g** | NET CARBS: **1g**

This recipe is an easy "master" recipe for marinating chicken with fresh herbs. With instructions for grilling, baking, and tips on using herbs other than the oregano in the shopping list, you can make this any way you want it. A few more amazingly versatile recipes like this, and this may just be the last cookbook I'll ever have to write!

Shopping List

1 tablespoon **olive oil**
1 tablespoon **white wine vinegar**
1 tablespoon chopped **fresh oregano**
1 teaspoon **minced garlic**
¾ teaspoon **salt**
¼ teaspoon **black pepper**
4 boneless, skinless chicken breasts

1. Add olive oil, white wine vinegar, fresh oregano, minced garlic, salt, and pepper to a large bowl and whisk until frothy.

2. Place chicken breasts in bowl and toss to coat. Cover and refrigerate to marinate at least 2 hours.

Grilled | Oil and then light or preheat a grill to medium-high to high. Remove chicken from marinade and grill until cooked through, about 4 minutes on each side. Serve garnished with fresh oregano.

Baked | Preheat the oven to 400 degrees and spray a sheet pan with nonstick cooking spray or lightly grease with olive oil. Remove chicken from marinade and bake on sheet pan for about 30 minutes, or until cooked through, and slicing into one reveals no pink. Serve garnished with fresh oregano.

George's Tips | This is even better when served topped with a fresh herb butter made by mixing ½ stick of soft butter or margarine with ½ teaspoon minced garlic, 1 tablespoon minced red onion, 1 tablespoon chopped fresh oregano, and a pinch of salt and pepper.

Variation | This can be done with any fresh herb, such as basil or thyme, but since Rachel has an herb garden, I really like a mixture of all three!

prep time	cook time	yield	serves
15 mins	12 mins	4 burgers	4

Chicken Cordon Bleu Burgers

calories: 350 | fat: 17g | protein: 43g | fiber: 0g | NET CARBS: 2g

Everyone loves Chicken Cordon Bleu, but even a chef like me can find the whole process of making it exhausting! This recipe takes all of the best components and puts them into a form anyone can make in minutes… a burger!

1. Combine all ingredients in a large bowl, mixing well. (It's easiest to use your hands.)

2. Form into 4, equal size patties. The thicker the patty, the longer the cook time will be, but less cheese will ooze out when cooking.

Shopping List

1 pound **ground chicken**
4 ounces **Swiss cheese**, cut into ½ inch cubes
½ cup diced **cooked ham**
¼ teaspoon **garlic powder**
¼ teaspoon **salt**
¼ teaspoon **black pepper**

3. Cook as you would normally cook a burger and serve with a knife and fork and all of the fixings, except the bun!

Pan Frying | Use a paper towel to evenly apply a small amount of vegetable oil to a nonstick frying or grill pan, and then place over medium-high heat. Let pan heat for 1 minute before placing burgers to cook. Cover and cook about 4-6 minutes on each side, or until burgers are well browned on the outside and white throughout. Some cheese will ooze out, so be sure to scrape it onto the burger before serving… it's the best part!

George's Tips | Raw ground chicken is very sticky; it's easiest to spray a little nonstick cooking spray on it, or even your hands, before forming the patties. When you don't have any leftover ham, most stores sell already diced ham cubes which are really convenient for this recipe.

Variation | I like to make a quick, sugar-free honey mustard sauce to serve with these by combining ¼ cup mayonnaise, 2 tablespoons brown deli-style mustard and 1 packet of sugar substitute.

Chicken Paprika Veldyne

calories: 400 | fat: 14g | protein: 57g | fiber: 2g | NET CARBS: 5g

My mother, Veldyne Stella, or "Val", was a great cook and my inspiration to become a chef. To me, she was Martha Stewart and Julia Child all in one. Hungarian cooking was just one of her favorites from goulash to kielbasa to this simple chicken paprika or as she would say, Paprikash.

1. Place margarine in a large skillet over medium-high heat.

2. Add chicken and lightly brown on each side, about 1-2 minutes per side.

3. Lower heat to medium and stir in onions, paprika, salt, and pepper, cooking 1 more minute.

Shopping List

2 tablespoons **trans-fat free margarine**

4 boneless, skinless chicken breasts, about 1½ pounds

1 cup sliced **yellow onion**

2 tablespoons **paprika**

½ teaspoon **salt**

¼ teaspoon **pepper**

½ cup **low sodium chicken broth**

8 ounces **light sour cream**, or **plain yogurt**

4. Pour in the chicken broth, cover, and simmer for 7-10 minutes more, or until chicken is cooked throughout and slicing into one reveals no pink.

5. Remove from heat and stir in sour cream. Serve hot garnished with a sprinkle of paprika.

George's Tips | Add 8 ounces of quartered mushrooms in step 3 and serve over some Awesome Grilled Asparagus, recipe page: 159, for a complete meal.

Variation | The sauce for this dish can be easily put together on its own to top any kind of meat. Simply skip step 2. Use the sauce to top fish, steak, and especially pork! Adding a dash of sherry is great for topping shrimp, crab, or even lobster!

prep time	marinate	cook time	serves
15 mins	1 hr	8 mins	4

Grilled Peach Chicken

calories: 300 | fat: 3g | protein: 55g | fiber: 1g | NET CARBS: 7g

Christian has been making this recipe for his wife for some time. I asked him how he came up with it and he said that he just wanted to find a way to make an entrée with grilled peaches after he photographed grilled peaches for an appetizer in my last book. Not only topped with grilled peach halves, the chicken itself is marinated in mashed peaches and teriyaki sauce for an entrée with tons of flavor in only 4 ingredients.

Shopping List

3 peaches
2 tablespoons **teriyaki sauce**
1 teaspoon **minced garlic**
4 **chicken breasts** (about 1½ pounds)

1. Slice 1 of the peaches in half, remove the pit, and add halves to a large bowl. Mash the halves with a potato masher or heavy spoon. Mash until you can remove any large pieces of the peach's peel by hand. (If you can't get it all, don't worry, you are only making a marinade.)

2. Add the teriyaki sauce and minced garlic to the mashed peach, and stir to combine. Place chicken breasts in marinade and toss to coat. Cover and refrigerate to marinate at least 1 hour.

3. Oil and then light or preheat a grill to medium-high to high. Cut remaining 2 peaches in half and remove their pits.

4. Remove chicken from marinade and grill until cooked through, about 4 minutes on each side. Grill peach halves alongside them, about 2 minutes on each side, or until nice grill marks have formed. Serve each chicken breast topped with one peach half.

George's Tips | Be sure to thoroughly oil the grill with nonstick cooking spray (before lighting!) or vegetable oil, before grilling to keep things from sticking. I like to lightly coat the peach halves in oil before grilling, just to be safe, as their natural sugars can stick easily.

Variation | Substitute 1 tablespoon of balsamic vinegar in place of the teriyaki sauce for another great flavor that goes well with peaches.

Lemon Pepper Turkey Breast

calories: 320 | fat: 7g | protein: 70g | fiber: 0g | NET CARBS: **3g**

Like pork, fresh turkey is finally getting accolades for being a healthy, low-fat, and high protein dinner option on more than just one day a year! We love making turkey breasts, as it's quicker than the whole bird and leaves us with just the right amount of leftovers. Because of that, we're always coming up with new ways to prepare them to keep things interesting, and this version with fresh lemon and fresh ground pepper is one of our absolute favorites!

1. Preheat the oven to 325 degrees and lightly coat a roasting pan with nonstick cooking spray.

2. To make a spice rub, place the margarine, lemon juice, lemon zest, salt, and pepper into a medium sized bowl and mix well.

Shopping List

nonstick cooking spray

3 tablespoons **trans-fat free margarine**, softened

2 tablespoons fresh **lemon juice**

1 teaspoon fresh **lemon zest**

¾ teaspoon **salt**

¼ teaspoon ground **black pepper**

5 to 7 pound **turkey breast**, bone-in

¼ teaspoon **paprika**

3. Place the turkey breast upright in the roasting pan, spread the entire bowl of rub evenly over the top, and then sprinkle with paprika.

4. Roast the turkey breast uncovered until it starts to turn golden brown. Loosely tent the breast with aluminum foil and finish cooking until thoroughly cooked with an internal temperature of at least 165 degrees. Depending on the size of the breast, the cooking time should be about 2 to 2 ½ hours, but use a meat thermometer to be safe! Let stand 10 minutes before carving.

George's Tips | For added flavor and flair, place slices of lemons over the top and hold them in place with toothpicks. And I like to put some celery stalks and quartered onions in the pan under the turkey for even more flavor AND to use as a simple roasted vegetable side!

Variation | Add 2 ounces of white wine, ¼ teaspoon of garlic, and a tablespoon of chopped parsley to the rub for a French Lemon-Pepper or "Francais" version! Or add 2 tablespoons fresh chopped dill, cilantro, basil, or even all 3 for a lemon herb turkey breast!

Chicken with Bacon, Tomato, and Thyme

Chicken with Bacon, Tomato, and Thyme

calories: 315 | fat: 15g | protein: 41g | fiber: 1g | NET CARBS: **2g**

This was one of my most popular recipes from my show on the Food Network. It just so happens to also be one of the easiest! In just a few ingredients you can make a top notch entrée that pairs well with just about any side dish.

1. Preheat the oven to 400 degrees and then partially cook the bacon by laying the slices on a baking sheet and baking for about 10 minutes. Transfer bacon to paper towels to drain. (You may use pre-cooked, store bought bacon and skip this step, though I find them thin and overly smoke flavored.)

2. Place chicken breasts in a large bowl and cover with olive oil, garlic, salt and pepper. Toss all to coat.

Shopping List

8 slices **bacon**

4 boneless, skinless chicken breasts

1 tablespoon **olive oil**

1 teaspoon **minced garlic**

⅛ teaspoon **salt**

⅛ teaspoon **black pepper**

2 **Roma tomatoes**

2 tablespoons chopped **red onion**

1 bunch **fresh thyme**

3. Transfer coated chicken breasts to a clean baking sheet and wrap each in 2 slices of bacon. The easiest way to do this is to crisscross the bacon, forming an X across the top of the breast, and tucking the ends of the bacon underneath the breasts.

4. Cut ends off Roma tomatoes and discard. Then cut each tomato into 2 thick slices.

5. Sprinkle chopped red onion evenly over chicken breasts, and then top each with a large sprig of thyme. Place 1 slice of the tomato in the center of each breast to hold the thyme in place. Bake in the 400 degree oven about 30 minutes, or until chicken is thoroughly cooked with an internal temperature of at least 180 degrees.

George's Tips | Gently pull the sprigs of thyme out from under the tomato before eating. I simply explain this to my guests after serving, as they make a far nicer presentation intact.

Variation | Skip step 1 and try substituting prosciutto (thin sliced, Italian ham) in place of the bacon, and fresh basil in place of the thyme!

prep time	cook time	serves
15 mins	75 mins	8

Cowboy Chili-Spiced Turkey Meatloaf

calories: 380 | fat: 18g | protein: 44g | fiber: 1g | NET CARBS: **2g**

Ground turkey makes a really great base for a creative meatloaf, especially this Southwestern one. The turkey really takes on the aromas of the chili powder, salsa, and Cheddar cheese that I use in place of breadcrumbs to create something entirely new and full of flavor.

1. Preheat oven to 350 degrees and ready a nonstick 9x5 loaf pan for baking. (Or spray a regular loaf pan with nonstick cooking spray.)

2. In a large bowl, mix the ground turkey, ½ cup of the salsa, eggs, Cheddar cheese, chili powder, salt, and pepper. (This is easiest done with your hands.)

Shopping List

2½ pounds **ground turkey**
1 cup **chunky salsa**
2 large **eggs**
1 cup shredded **sharp Cheddar cheese**
1 tablespoon **chili powder**
¾ teaspoon **salt**
¼ teaspoon **black pepper**

3. Fill loaf pan with the meatloaf mixture, patting with your hands to form an even top. Cover the meatloaf with the remaining ½ cup of salsa and bake uncovered for 75 minutes or until a meat thermometer registers 165 degrees.

4. Drain any excess grease from pan and let rest 10 minutes before cutting into 8 equal slices.

George's Tips | There are many varieties of ground turkey available these days. I like to use lean ground turkey with about 12g of fat per serving, but not the extremely lean ground turkey breast with only 2-4g of fat per serving as it tends to dry out no matter how you cook it.

Variation | This mix also makes great Turkey Burgers, simply form into 8 patties and pan fry, or grill until cutting into one reveals that it is cooked throughout. Just remember to only use the ½ cup of salsa in the mix and skip the other ½ cup of salsa used to top the meatloaf.

Meats

Not Your Mother's Beef Stroganoff

calories: 475 | fat: 26g | protein: 41g | fiber: 4g | NET CARBS: **13g**

Beef stroganoff is an absolute classic comfort food that pretty much everyone grew up eating. With that said, it is with great caution that I throw tradition to the wind and present this new spin on stroganoff featuring spinach and tomatoes in place of the usual mushrooms.

1. Place margarine in a large skillet over medium-high to high heat and heat until sizzling.

2. Add sirloin slices and brown well on both sides, 2-3 minutes per side.

3. Lower heat to medium, stir in fresh spinach, cherry tomatoes, minced garlic, tarragon, salt, and pepper and cook an additional minute, just until spinach begins to wilt.

4. Remove from heat and stir in sour cream, mixing until melted and well combined. Serve over spaghetti squash or whole wheat noodles, garnished with fresh tarragon or parsley.

George's Tips | See my recipe for Spaghetti Squash with Ricotta Blush Sauce, recipe page: 147, for instructions on how to prepare a spaghetti squash to serve this over.

Variation | For a less expensive alternative, substitute 1 pound of ground beef or turkey for the top sirloin, though then I would suggest draining off some of the grease before adding the spinach in step 3.

Shopping List

2 tablespoons **trans-fat free margarine**

1 pound **top sirloin**, cut into ⅓ inch thick slices

3 packed cups **fresh spinach leaves**

12 cherry tomatoes, halved

2 teaspoons **minced garlic**

2 teaspoons chopped **fresh tarragon**

½ teaspoon **salt**

¼ teaspoon **pepper**

16 ounces light sour cream

Meats

prep time	cook time	serves
10 mins	1.5 hrs	8

Herb Roasted Pork Loin

calories: 355 | fat: 11g | protein: 60g | fiber: 0g | NET CARBS: **0g**

I have carved many a whole pork loin or beef tenderloin in my time. Always dressed in full chef uniform and carving at a station on the buffet, I found that herb roasted whole pork loin has been the hit of large catered events since I first started doing them. Chefs like it because you can prep it in just a few minutes, pop it in the oven, and then move on to something else without having to worry.

Shopping List

nonstick cooking spray
1 boneless pork loin, about 4 pounds
2 tablespoons **olive oil**
2 tablespoons chopped **fresh basil**
2 tablespoons chopped **fresh cilantro**
1 tablespoon **kosher salt**
½ teaspoon **black pepper**
¼ teaspoon **garlic powder**

1. Preheat the oven to 350 degrees and spray a shallow roasting pan with nonstick cooking spray.

2. Coat the loin with the olive oil, sprinkle with the remaining ingredients, and then rub all into the pork.

3. Place the seasoned pork loin in the pan and bake for 20 minutes.

4. Reduce the heat to 300 degrees and continue baking for about 1 hour, until a meat thermometer stuck into the thickest part of the loin registers 145 degrees.

5. Remove the pork loin from the oven and let rest for at least 10 minutes before slicing.

George's Tips | This recipe is so great for parties because you can make it ahead of time by undercooking it to 130 degrees, cool or refrigerate, and reheat slowly up to 145 degrees just before serving! Also, if cilantro isn't your thing, you can easily substitute parsley.

Variation | Try cutting the loin into double thick boneless center cut pork chops and grilling instead! Simply cut the raw loin into steaks, as thick as you want them. Coat each with the seasonings and grill over medium-high heat for about 5 minutes on each side. (More or less depending on thickness of steaks cut.)

Grilled Italian Marinated London Broil

calories: 425 | fat: 11g | protein: 67g | fiber: 0g | NET CARBS: **2g**

We chefs take short cuts like the one in this recipe all the time to add layers of flavors to what is otherwise just a simple cut of meat. Why chop garlic and onions and measure seasonings when all you have to do is use a bottle of good Italian dressing to get almost all of the same flavors? Just be sure to look for a high quality dressing that is very low in sugar; I like Newman's Own.

Shopping List

1 bottle (16-ounce) **Italian salad dressing**
½ teaspoon **salt**
¼ teaspoon **black pepper**
2½ pounds **London broil steak**, may use sirloin

1. Place all the ingredients, including the steak, into a large food storage container or baking dish with lid.

2. Marinate the steak in the refrigerator for at least 1 hour and up to overnight.

3. When ready to cook, oil and then light or preheat a grill to high. Or place an indoor cast-iron grill pan over medium-high heat.

4. Remove the steak from the container and discard the used marinade.

5. Place the London broil on the grill and cook for about 7-8 minutes on each side, turning once or twice until cooked medium rare, or when a meat thermometer stuck in the thickest part registers 145 degrees. Let rest 5 minutes before slicing. Thinly slice against the grain of the meat to serve.

George's Tips | Although the marinade is flavorful enough, you can also serve with one of my Three Creamy Steak Sauces, recipe page: 103.

Variation | I like to throw some whole baby bella or button mushrooms in the marinade with the steak to marinate and then grill alongside it. Simply grill them along the outer, cooler edges of the grill as the steak is cooking and everything should be ready at the same time.

Meats

Marinara + Mozzarella Meatloaf

calories: 425 | fat: 28g | protein: 29g | fiber: 1g | NET CARBS: **6.5g**

This recipe for an Italian meatloaf opts for marinara sauce instead of ketchup, which goes extremely well with my secret ingredient for making juicy meatloaves without breadcrumbs—Parmesan cheese. Once you top with the Mozzarella cheese, you've pretty much got "Meatloaf Parmesan", but I like the three M's in my title better!

1. Preheat oven to 350 degrees and ready a nonstick 9x5 loaf pan for baking. (Or spray a regular loaf pan with nonstick cooking spray.)

2. In a large bowl, mix the ground beef, 1 cup of the marinara sauce, diced red onion, eggs, Parmesan cheese, Italian seasoning, and salt and pepper. (This is easiest done with your hands.)

Shopping List

2 pounds **lean ground beef**
1½ cups **marinara sauce**
¼ cup diced **red onion**
3 large **eggs**
½ cup grated **Parmesan cheese**
1 teaspoon **Italian seasoning**
½ teaspoon each of **salt** and **pepper**
¾ cup **mozzarella cheese**

3. Evenly fill loaf pan with the meatloaf mixture, patting with your hands to form an even top. Bake uncovered for 45 minutes.

4. Remove loaf from oven, drain any excess fat or liquid, and then top with the remaining ½ cup of marinara sauce, and all of the mozzarella cheese. Return to oven and bake an additional 30 minutes, or until a meat thermometer registers 165 degrees. Drain fat from pan once more and let rest 10 minutes before cutting into 8 equal slices.

George's Tips | When buying marinara sauce, it is very important to read the labels! Look for the sauce that is the lowest in sugar. While tomatoes contain some natural sugars, check the ingredients list for any sugar or corn syrup that may have been added. With so many jars to choose from, there's no need to buy the one with added corn syrup!

Variation | If you do not have a loaf pan, simply form a rounded loaf by hand in a large baking dish. Also, you can make an Italian Vegetable Stuffed Meatloaf by adding ¼ cup of diced roasted red peppers and ½ cup of diced fresh zucchini.

Meats

prep time 10 mins	cook time 45 mins	serving 2 chops	serves 4

Family Favorite Baked Pork Chops

calories: 678 | fat: 30g | protein: 94g | fiber: 0g | NET CARBS: **0.5g**

We are big on just seasoning something well and throwing it in the oven. It's our kind of comfort food. Usually it's some kind of chicken on sale that we are throwing in the baking dish, but lately pork IS the NEW chicken, and pork of any kind is almost always a great deal, even at regular price!

1. Preheat the oven to 375 degrees and spray a sheet pan with nonstick cooking spray.

2. Place the pork chops in the pan in a single layer and sprinkle evenly with remaining ingredients.

Shopping List

nonstick cooking spray
8 bone-in pork chops, about **3** pounds
¾ teaspoon **salt**
½ teaspoon **black pepper**
1 teaspoon **dried oregano**
⅛ teaspoon **garlic powder**
½ teaspoon **paprika**

3. Bake for 40-45 minutes, until tender. Serve garnished with fresh lemon wedges and parsley if desired.

George's Tips | Place a few veggies in the oven to roast right alongside the chops. Quartered onions, button or baby bella mushrooms, and celery sticks go perfectly with the meal!

Variation | You can use the exact same seasonings and method to cook chicken leg quarters (which are usually on sale VERY cheap), about 45-50 minutes at 375 degrees, until the juices run clear.

Meats

Three Creamy Steak Sauces

These are three recipes for quick and easy steak sauces that you can whip together in an instant the next time that you are preparing steak. You've got two cold sauces—one with horseradish and one with Dijon—and a third sauce with Gorgonzola that is served warm, drizzled over the steak. All three are quite strong though, so remember that a little goes a long way here!

Shopping List

HORSERADISH CREAM SAUCE

1 cup **sour cream**
2 tablespoons prepared **horseradish**
1 teaspoon **lemon juice**

CREAMY DIJON MUSTARD SAUCE

½ cup **light mayonnaise**
½ cup **Dijon mustard**
1 teaspoon **lemon juice**
1 teaspoon **bulk sugar substitute**

GORGONZOLA CREAM SAUCE

⅔ cup **gorgonzola**, or any **bleu cheese**
¼ cup **mayonnaise**
dash **Worcestershire sauce**
¼ teaspoon ground **black pepper**

Horseradish Cream Sauce

calories: 40 | fat: 4g | NET CARBS: 1g

1. Add all ingredients to a serving bowl and mix well. (You may wish to add additional horseradish to taste, depending on the strength of the horseradish being used.)

Creamy Dijon Mustard Sauce

calories: 20 | fat: 2g | NET CARBS: 1g

1. Add all ingredients to a serving bowl and mix well.

Gorgonzola Cream Sauce

calories: 50 | fat: 4g | NET CARBS: 1g

1. Add all ingredients to a small sauce pan over medium heat. Stir constantly until gorgonzola cheese melts and all ingredients are combined and creamy. Serve warm, over top steaks.

Variation | Light sour cream can be used in place of the regular sour cream in the Horseradish Cream Sauce, though it will not be as thick. Light mayonnaise is already used in the Dijon sauce, but I would not recommend using light mayonnaise in the Gorgonzola sauce, as the fat helps hold the sauce together.

Meats

prep time	cook time	serves
15 mins	6 mins	4

Grilled Ham Steaks with Peach Chutney

calories: 290 | fat: 14g | protein: 28g | fiber: 3g | NET CARBS: **7g**

Sometimes, it's hard to think of what to do with a good ham steak! I mean, they're so good grilled that you don't need to improve upon them very much. In lieu of any kind of sugary glaze, this recipe uses a peach chutney that not only adds beautiful colors to the plate, but a much fresher flavor. Fresh peaches are best (when they're ripe), but they were out of season the last time we made this (and photographed it to the left) and we found that the frozen peach slices were much easier to cut (as they have no skin) and tasted pretty darn good… so we re-wrote the recipe!

Shopping List

¾ cup **frozen peach slices**
2 tablespoons diced **green bell pepper**
1 tablespoon diced **red onion**
1 teaspoon **bulk sugar substitute**
2 large **ham steaks**

1. Oil and then light or preheat a grill to medium-high to high.

2. Dice peach slices into small cubes. You can make cleaner, more precise cuts while peaches are still somewhat frozen.

3. Add peach cubes to a bowl with the diced green bell pepper, diced red onion, and sugar substitute and stir to combine. Let sit out to continue thawing while you prepare the ham steaks.

4. Grill ham steaks about 3 minutes on each side, just until well seared and hot all the way through. Serve alongside or topped with chutney.

George's Tips | Bone-in ham steaks are best, as usually the boneless ones are nothing more than thick cut, processed lunch meat. The chutney also goes well with traditional baked ham.

Variation | Make a peach glaze for the ham by thawing ½ cup frozen peach slices and adding to a food processor with 3 teaspoons of low sodium teriyaki sauce. Puree until smooth and brush onto ham steaks before grilling.

Swedish Meatballs

calories: 395 | fat: 18g | protein: 30g | fiber: 0g | NET CARBS: **3g**

These are slightly spiced Swedish Meatballs in a creamy sour cream sauce, the same way my mother made them for me when I was a kid, just without the white flour breadcrumbs that add nothing to the flavor anyway.

1. Prepare the meatballs by combining all Meatball ingredients in a large mixing bowl. Use your hands to mix well and form into slightly smaller than golf ball sized meatballs.

2. Place margarine in a large skillet over medium-high heat. Add meatballs and brown well, about 3-4 minutes.

3. Add the beef base and ½ cup of tap water, and simmer for 5 minutes more.

4. Remove from heat and stir in sour cream. Serve hot, over cooked spaghetti squash, steamed cauliflower, or whole wheat noodles. Garnish with fresh parsley.

Shopping List

MEATBALLS

1 pound **ground beef**
1 **egg**
¼ cup finely minced **onion**
¼ teaspoon **salt**
¼ teaspoon **white pepper**
¼ teaspoon **allspice**

SAUCE

2 tablespoons **trans-fat free margarine**
1 teaspoon **beef base**
8 ounces **light sour cream**

George's Tips | Ground cinnamon can be used in place of the allspice if that is all you have on hand, though allspice has a more interesting variety of flavors. Though it isn't necessary, I like to add 2 teaspoons of parsley flakes or fresh chopped parsley to the meatball mix to give them little specks of color.

Variation | You can also substitute 1 pound of ground turkey for the beef. Leave out the egg, double the allspice, and add all of the meatball ingredients to the pan in step 2 without forming into balls—crumbling the ground beef with a spatula as it browns—to make a Spiced Ground Beef Stroganoff.

Meats

Steak Pizzaiola

calories: 530 | fat: 23g | protein: 60g | fiber: 2g | NET CARBS: **1.5g**

This is the first recipe I ever made when I was 7 or 8 years old. I found it in one of my mom's old recipe books. I remember proudly spending an entire day prepping and preparing it exactly to the recipe and serving it to my parents and sisters! When I look at how simple this recipe really is today, I can only wonder what I did all day back then to take so long making it!

Shopping List

2 tablespoons **olive oil**
1 cup sliced **yellow onion**
1½ pounds **beef sirloin**, cut into strips
½ teaspoon **salt**
⅛ teaspoon **black pepper**
1½ cups **marinara sauce**
1 cup shredded **mozzarella cheese**

Meats

1. Heat the oil in a large skillet over medium-high heat.

2. Add the onion, steak, salt and black pepper and cook for about 5 minutes, or until the steak strips are cooked. Turn the heat off.

3. Mix the marinara sauce into the cooked steak and top with the cheese. Cover skillet for about 2 minutes to let the cheese melt. Serve hot as a main dish or if you desire serve over whole wheat pasta or spaghetti squash.

George's Tips | Adding a teaspoon of fresh chopped or roasted garlic will give this dish a little zing!

Variation | This is also great with chicken cut into strips in place of the beef! You can also top with classic pizza toppings such as sliced mushrooms or even pepperoni to spice it up a bit!

Grilled Sirloin Marsala

calories: 435 | fat: 19g | protein: 53g | fiber: 1g | NET CARBS: **3g**

Christian has been really adamant that some of my classic recipes have unnecessary ingredients, and that simpler is better. He pointed to the Chicken Marsala recipe in my last book and how it had 15 ingredients! I set out to write this Grilled Sirloin Marsala for vindication, and I couldn't believe how amazing the sauce turned out using only 5 ingredients!

Shopping List

2-4 **sirloin steaks**
8 ounces **baby bella mushrooms**
2 tablespoons **trans-fat free margarine**
¼ cup **Marsala wine**
½ cup **heavy cream**
½ teaspoon **beef base**

1. Trim about half the length of the mushrooms' stems and discard, and then quarter mushrooms.

2. Cook margarine in a sauté pan over medium-high heat until sizzling. Add mushrooms and cook for 1 minute before adding the Marsala wine and cooking 1 minute further.

3. Stir cream and beef base into the pan with mushrooms, and continue cooking until sauce has reduced enough to coat the back of a spoon, about 4 minutes. Serve smothered over a sirloin (or any kind of) steak for each person. Makes enough sauce for 4 steaks, but you can refrigerate leftover sauce if only cooking for 2.

Grilling Sirloins | Oil and then light or preheat a grill to medium-high to high. Season both sides of steaks with salt and pepper before grilling. Grill ¾ inch sirloins about 5 minutes on each side for medium rare. Medium well will take about 8 minutes on each side. For thicker steaks, add 2-4 minutes.

George's Tips | Beef base is sold in small jars near the bouillon cubes in the grocery store and has a lot more flavor than bouillon cubes. In a pinch, you can substitute 1 bouillon cube in this recipe. You can also substitute regular white button mushrooms for the baby bellas.

Variation | To broil sirloins: spray a broiler pan with nonstick cooking spray, season both sides of steaks with salt and pepper, and broil 3-4 minutes on each side for ¾ inch steaks that are medium rare. Add 2-3 minutes for medium well.

Szechuan Beef and Broccoli

calories: 290 | fat: 14g | protein: 36g | fiber: 1g | NET CARBS: **2.5g**

Stir fry is about the easiest one pan meal around which is why I've included several in this book. What sets this one apart is that this Szechuan inspired take on Beef and Broccoli is hot and spicy, so don't say I didn't warn you. (I might have warned you, but I also came up with the recipe, so I guess the blame is still on me!)

1. Heat the sesame oil in a sauté pan or wok over medium-high heat until sizzling. Add steak strips and broccoli florets, and cook without stirring for 1-2 minutes, until they begin to brown. Stir once and continue cooking another 1-2 minutes to brown them further.

Shopping List

2 tablespoons **sesame oil**

1 pound **beef sirloin**, cut into strips

2 cups **fresh broccoli**, cut into small florets

2 tablespoons **soy sauce**

1 teaspoon **chopped garlic**

¼ teaspoon **ground ginger**

⅛ teaspoon **crushed red pepper**, or **cayenne pepper**

2. Add remaining ingredients to pan, stir all to combine and cook for 1-2 more minutes, or until the broccoli is as tender as you would like it. (It's best somewhat crunchy in this!)

3. Remove from heat and serve garnished with roasted red peppers or sesame seeds, if you desire.

George's Tips | For a richer beef taste you can add in a teaspoon of beef base, such as Better than Bouillon, sold in small jars near the beef broth. You can also use any oil in place of the sesame oil, if you don't have any on hand, though sesame oil will add a great flavor.

Variation | You can also make this using chicken or pork! Add sliced zucchini, yellow squash, and baby bella mushrooms after the first 2 minutes of browning the meat for a feast fit for a king! Adding 1 tablespoon of honey will give you a sweet and spicy sauce, similar to some of the sugar filled sauces of Chinese takeout.

Seafood

| Sesame Crusted Salmon

prep time	cook time	serves
10 mins	9 mins	4

Sesame Crusted Salmon

calories: 380 | fat: 20g | protein: 45g | fiber: 1g | NET CARBS: **1g**

This salmon looks and tastes like something out of a cutting edge restaurant, but is amazingly easy to make. You don't have to mix up a dozen ingredients to make a beautifully crusted fish, you just have to flip it into the pan and leave it alone until the crust cooks itself into the fish... so while this dish is real pretty to look at... don't touch! (Until the crust is browned and in place, of course.)

Shopping List

1 tablespoon **sesame oil**

3 or more tablespoons **sesame seeds**

1½ pounds skinless **salmon**, cut into **4** fillets

1 tablespoon **soy sauce**

1. Add the sesame oil to a large nonstick skillet over medium-high to high heat.

2. Spread sesame seeds across the surface of a dinner plate and then press one side of each salmon fillet into them to coat. Transfer coated fillets to the hot skillet, placing them seed side down.

3. Cook salmon until the sesame seed crust browns, about 3-4 minutes. Flip salmon and cook an additional minute before adding the soy sauce.

4. Reduce heat to medium and cook salmon in soy sauce for 2-4 more minutes or until a light pink color throughout. Serve over a stir fry, with soy sauce and wasabi, or with one of the dipping sauces in the variation below.

George's Tips | Use both white and black (if they are available) sesame seeds for a nice contrast in the crust.

Variation | Make a Teriyaki Mayonnaise for dipping by combining ¼ cup light mayonnaise with 1 tablespoon teriyaki sauce. Or make a Honey Garlic Mayonnaise with ¼ cup light mayonnaise, 1 tablespoon honey, 1 teaspoon minced garlic, and 2 teaspoons soy sauce.

| Rocky Point Clam Cakes

prep time	cook time	yield	serves
10 mins	15 mins	24 cakes	8

Rocky Point Clam Cakes

calories: 235 | fat: 15g | protein: 10.5g | fiber: 2.5g | NET CARBS: **11g**

Almost 30 years ago Rachel took me to an amusement park in Rhode Island called Rocky Point. She had many comforting memories of going to that place as a kid, and she had to take me to it and show me. The first place we HAD to go was their gigantic "Mess Hall" that seated thousands and where they served the world famous Rocky Point Clam Cakes. The only difference in ours from theirs is that we put in 10 times more clams; because we can!

Shopping List

4-6 cups **vegetable oil**, for frying
1-10 ounce can **baby clams** in water
¾ cup **whole wheat flour**
¾ cup **soy flour**
2 large **eggs**
1 tablespoon **baking powder**
1 teaspoon **salt**
½ teaspoon **black pepper**
¼ teaspoon **garlic powder**

1. Place a pot over medium-high heat and fill with at least 3 inches of vegetable oil. Heat oil until about 350 degrees, about 5 minutes.

2. In a large bowl, combine entire contents of canned clams including the water with all ingredients until a thick, but smooth consistency is reached.

3. With a teaspoon, drop walnut sized amounts of the batter gently into the hot oil, being careful not to splash.

4. Fry the clam cakes in small batches of 4 or 5 for about 3 minutes each batch or until deep golden brown. Let rest on paper towels to drain excess oil before serving hot. Garnish with lemon wedges for the perfect presentation!

George's Tips | The batter should be sticky and "spoonable". If it seems too thick, simply add a little water, and if too thin add a little flour.

Variation | This "fritter" batter is a perfect base for just about anything! In place of clams try crab, chopped conch, diced ham and pimentos, leftover shredded rotisserie chicken—you get the idea!

Seafood

Grilled Dill Shrimp

calories: 228 | fat: 6.5g | protein: 41g | fiber: 0g | NET CARBS: **1.5g**

When it comes to grilling, you can't get much quicker than shrimp, and when it comes to grilled shrimp, you can't get much easier than this recipe! With a flash marinade in dill, olive oil, and garlic, the best flavors come to those who don't have to wait!

1. In a large bowl, combine shrimp and all other ingredients, tossing to coat. Refrigerate for only 10 minutes to marinate. (Any longer and the acidity of the lemon juice will cook the shrimp.)

2. Oil and then light or preheat a grill to medium.

Shopping List

2 pounds **jumbo shrimp**, peeled and deveined

3 tablespoons **olive oil**

2 rounded teaspoons **minced garlic**

1 tablespoon finely chopped **fresh dill**

juice of ½ **lemon**

½ teaspoon **salt**

⅛ teaspoon **black pepper**

3. Toss shrimp in marinade one last time and then grill about 2-3 minutes on each side, until just cooked all the way through. Shrimp will turn from translucent blue to white and pink once cooked. Serve garnished with fresh dill and lemon wedges.

Making as Skewers | Make party shrimp skewers by soaking bamboo skewers in water for 30 minutes before grilling and then threading each shrimp onto a skewer before placing on the grill.

George's Tips | Cooking times are approximate for large shrimp, sold about 12-15 to a pound. Shrimp sold 16-20 to a pound will cook in less than 2 minutes on each side.

Variation | This is even better when served topped with a fresh dill butter made by mixing ½ stick of soft butter or margarine with 1 teaspoon minced garlic, 1 tablespoon minced red onion, 1 tablespoon chopped fresh dill, and a pinch of salt and pepper.

Seafood

Bronzed Salmon

calories: 370 | fat: 19g | protein: 43g | fiber: 0g | NET CARBS: **0g**

This salmon recipe uses a classic fish preparation known as "bronzing". It's a surefire way to make fish that is full of flavor, without entirely "blackening" the fish with seasoning (like I'm known to do). Though I've used Old Bay here for something nice and mild, you can use any of your favorite seasoning blends, including my very own Blackening Spice, recipe at the bottom of the page.

Shopping List

1 tablespoon **olive oil**

1½ pounds **salmon**, cut into **4** fillets

1½ tablespoons **Old Bay seasoning**

¼ cup **white wine** (may use chicken broth)

1 tablespoon **trans-fat free margarine**

1. Add the olive oil to a large nonstick skillet over medium-high to high heat. Once sizzling, add salmon fillets.

2. Cook salmon until bottom browns, about 3-4 minutes. Flip salmon and season the browned top liberally with the Old Bay seasoning. Reduce heat to medium and cover pan, cooking 1 minute.

3. Add white wine and margarine and cook an additional 2 minutes or until salmon is cooked and a light pink color throughout. Serve garnished with fresh lemon wedges and drizzled with the liquid from the pan.

George's Tips | If using chicken broth in place of the white wine, I'd highly recommend squeezing the juice of ½ of a lemon into the pan at the same time to replace the acidity of the wine.

Variation | You can also use 1½ tablespoons of Blackening Spice in place of the Old Bay seasoning for a spicier, totally different flavor.

Blackening Spice | Make a large batch of my famous blackening spice by combining 5 tablespoons kosher salt, 5 tablespoons paprika, 1 tablespoon dry thyme, 1 tablespoon black pepper, 1 tablespoon garlic powder, ½ teaspoon cayenne pepper, and ½ teaspoon white pepper.

Honey Lime Tilapia

calories: 160 | fat: 1.5g | protein: 32g | fiber: 0g | NET CARBS: **5g**

When cooking seafood, especially tilapia, you've really got to keep things simple... which fits right into the idea behind this book. (That's convenient!) Simple, fresh flavors like honey, cilantro, and lime are just bold enough, without overpowering the extremely mild fish. I simply don't know what I'll do with seafood if my next book is about making things complicated. (It won't be!)

Shopping List

nonstick cooking spray
1½ pounds **tilapia fillets**
juice of **1** large **lime**
1 tablespoon **honey**
1 tablespoon fresh chopped **cilantro**
1 teaspoon **minced garlic**
¼ teaspoon **salt**

1. Preheat the oven to 375 degrees and generously spray a sheet pan with nonstick cooking spray. (Or coat with 1 tablespoon of olive oil for even more flavor!) Place tilapia fillets on greased sheet pan.

2. Add remaining ingredients to a small bowl, mix well, and then drizzle over tilapia fillets evenly.

3. Bake for 15 minutes, or until fish begins to turn a light brown and easily flakes with a fork. Serve basted with the juices in the pan, garnished with fresh lime and cilantro.

George's Tips | For even more flavor, gently toss the fish in a bowl with the sauce and then marinate in the refrigerator for 10 minutes as the oven preheats. Just don't let it marinate more than 20 minutes, as the acid in the lime juice will begin to break down the texture of the fish.

Variation | Turn these into Lemon Herb Tilapia Fillets by replacing the honey with white wine, the lime juice with lemon juice, and the cilantro with fresh herbs like oregano or thyme.

Seafood

Easy Steamed Clams

calories: 255 | fat: 14g | protein: 9g | fiber: 0g | NET CARBS: **6g**

Cooking seafood can be intimidating to a lot of people, but there really isn't anything easier than steaming clams in a simple broth like this recipe. You throw a little garlic, onion, and wine in a pot with some fresh clams, cover, and in less than 10 minutes you've made clams with a broth that rivals any restaurant!

Shopping List

3 tablespoons **trans-fat free margarine**

1 tablespoon **minced garlic**

2 tablespoons diced **red onion**

¾ cup **white wine**

2 pounds **fresh clams**, washed

salt and **pepper**

1. Add the margarine to a large nonstick skillet or pot over medium-high heat. Once sizzling, add the garlic and onion and cook 1 minute.

2. Add the white wine and clams to the skillet, reduce heat to medium, and cover tightly.

3. Cook 5-10 minutes, shaking the pan occasionally to keep things moving, until all or almost all of the clams have opened. Discard unopened clams. Salt and pepper the broth to taste and serve clams drizzled in it and garnished with fresh parsley.

George's Tips | Clams should be washed and scrubbed with a coarse brush before cooking to ensure the least amount of grit getting into the broth. Any clams that are open before cooking have died and should be discarded.

Variation | Though the alcohol will cook out in the cooking process, you can substitute vegetable broth or clam juice (sold in skinny bottles near the canned clams) for the wine. I would also squeeze a few teaspoons of fresh lemon juice into the dish to bring a little acidity that you would lose without the wine.

Seafood

Tuna and Chickpea Salad

calories: 175 | fat: 5g | protein: 16.5g | fiber: 5g | NET CARBS: **12g**

I've always loved a scoop of cold tuna salad atop a fresh bed of lettuce, but traditional tuna salads are a little lacking in the texture department. This recipe adds not only the texture of chickpeas, but the protein, fiber, and calcium (almost as much as milk!) that come along with them.

Shopping List

½ cup **canned chickpeas**, drained
1 can (**6** ounces) **albacore tuna**, drained
⅓ cup **light mayonnaise** (or regular)
¼ cup chopped **celery**
1 tablespoon diced **yellow onion**
2 teaspoons **Dijon mustard**
¼ teaspoon **salt**

1. Fold all ingredients together in a large bowl, flaking tuna with a fork to break up any large pieces (unless you prefer it chunky).

2. Cover and refrigerate for 30 minutes for the ingredients and flavors to mingle, or serve immediately. Serve over a green salad, if desired. Garnish with a sprinkle of paprika or fresh parsley, and a wedge of fresh lemon.

George's Tips | I like to use the pouches of tuna that have popped up in stores over the last few years. They just taste fresher! I also like to thoroughly rinse canned chickpeas before using them, as the canning brine will overpower the other ingredients in the salad.

Variation | Use an entire can of chickpeas and skip the tuna for a vegetarian salad that still packs protein. This is also a really good option for expectant mothers that are watching their fish intake. You can also use garbanzo beans to make this recipe—just kidding, chickpeas are garbanzo beans!

Turkey Bacon Wrapped Scallops

calories: 80 | fat: 2g | protein: 12.5g | fiber: 0g | NET CARBS: **1.5g**

Bacon wrapped scallops are an easy and impressive appetizer, but the bacon is all too often chewy and undercooked. Making them with turkey bacon is not only healthier, but far easier to (literally) sink your teeth into without all of the fat of regular bacon needing to crisp up—but don't worry, turkey bacon still gets plenty crispy.

Shopping List

8 slices **turkey bacon**
16 **sea scallops** (about 1 pound)
2 teaspoons **olive oil**
2 teaspoons **lemon juice**
¼ teaspoon **salt**
⅛ teaspoon **black pepper**

1. Preheat the oven to 420 degrees. Cook turkey bacon in a nonstick skillet over medium-high heat about 5 minutes, flipping halfway through. Only cook the bacon until very lightly browned, not fully done. Transfer to paper towels and cut each piece in half, crosswise. Set aside.

2. Place scallops and remaining ingredients in a large bowl and toss all to coat.

3. Wrap the circumference of each coated scallop in a piece of the cut bacon, securing the bacon by skewering through it and the entire scallop with a toothpick. Repeat with each scallop, placing the skewered ones on a baking sheet.

4. Bake for 10-12 minutes or until scallops look more plump and give a little bounce and resistance when poking the top with a finger. Serve on a platter, garnished with fresh parsley and lemon wedges.

George's Tips | These are even better on the grill. Soak larger bamboo skewers for 30 minutes before threading 3 bacon wrapped scallops onto each skewer. Grill skewers for about 3 minutes on each side.

Variation | You can also make these with regular bacon by frying the bacon by adding about 2 minutes to the frying time of the bacon before wrapping. The easiest way to make these with regular bacon is to skip frying the bacon altogether and wrap the scallops in cold, store-bought pre-cooked bacon before baking.

Seafood

Salmon with a Creamy Dill Sauce

calories: 385 | fat: 20g | protein: 44g | fiber: 0g | NET CARBS: **1.5g**

This recipe takes me back to my first years working in restaurants, but just because it's an oldie, doesn't mean this wheel isn't round! The classics have become classics for many reasons, but one reason is that they're easy to prepare. Chefs don't like to take something this quick, easy, and delicious off the menu!

Shopping List

2 tablespoons **trans-fat free margarine**

1½ pounds **salmon**, cut into 4 fillets

salt and **pepper**

½ fresh **lemon**

1½ tablespoons fresh chopped **dill**

¼ cup **heavy cream**

2 teaspoons **Dijon mustard**

1. Add the margarine to a large nonstick skillet over medium-high to high heat. Once sizzling, add salmon fillets. Generously season the top of the salmon with salt and pepper.

2. Cook salmon until bottom browns, about 3-4 minutes. Flip salmon and squeeze the juice out of the ½ lemon over top all fillets.

3. Add ¼ cup of tap water, reduce heat to medium, and cover pan, cooking about 3 minutes or until salmon is cooked and a light pink color throughout.

4. Transfer salmon to a serving platter. Add dill, heavy cream, and Dijon mustard to the cooking liquid in the skillet and stir to create the sauce. Drizzle sauce over the salmon and serve garnished with fresh dill.

George's Tips | 1½ teaspoons of dry dill weed can be used in place of the fresh dill, but fresh is definitely best in this case.

Variation | You can use ½ cup of reduced fat sour cream in place of the heavy cream to lower the fat in this recipe, but don't forget that though this recipe seems to be high in fat, a good amount of that fat is the heart healthy fat found in salmon!

Seafood

Slow Cooker Cookery

Cabbage and Kielbasa Soup

calories: 250 | fat: 16.5g | protein: 15g | fiber: 2g | NET CARBS: **7g**

Polish sausage and cabbage are a tried and true combination that can't go wrong, especially in this stupendously simple soup. Leave it in the slow cooker while you're out, or just cover and simmer it on the stove for 45 minutes if you simply can't wait. (I know this is the slow cooker section of the book, but I usually want this soup NOW.)

1. Slice kielbasa into discs, about ⅓ inch thick. Add olive oil and kielbasa to a large skillet over medium-high to high heat, browning well, about 3 minutes each side. When meat is almost browned, add onions to cook just until they sweat.

Shopping List

16 ounces **kielbasa sausage**

1 tablespoon **olive oil**

1 medium **onion**, chopped

6 cups **chicken broth**

4 cups shredded **cabbage**

1 large **bay leaf**

½ teaspoon **black pepper**

2. Transfer kielbasa and onions to a slow cooker set to low. Add some of the chicken broth to the skillet the kielbasa was cooked in and use a spatula to scrape the bottom, breaking up any glaze the kielbasa may have left in the pan. Pour over kielbasa and onions in slow cooker, and then pour in remaining chicken broth.

3. Add the cabbage, bay leaf, and black pepper to the cooker and stir all to combine.

4. Cover and let cook 4-6 hours, depending on when you are ready to serve. Remove bay leaf and serve. Depending on the sodium content of the chicken broth and kielbasa, you may want to add salt to taste before serving. Garnish with fresh parsley, if desired.

George's Tips | While buying a head of green cabbage and shredding yourself will be cheaper, you can purchase a bag of shredded coleslaw cabbage in the bagged salad mix section to save time. Buying "Better Than Bouillon" chicken base, sold in jars near the cartons of broth, and mixing 6 teaspoons with 6 cups water will save you from having to purchase so much broth.

Variation | Turkey kielbasa can be used in place of the regular kielbasa to lower the fat in this recipe. Adding 2 tablespoons of apple cider vinegar will give the soup more depth, adding a little sweet and a little sour… two things that go very well with cabbage.

Slow Cooker

prep time	cook time	serves
20 mins	5+ hrs	4-6

Chicken in Broccoli Cheese Sauce

calories: 460 | fat: 19g | protein: 63g | fiber: 1g | NET CARBS: 4g

Getting children to eat vegetables may be quite a task, but I think we all know that children will eat broccoli when there's a cheese sauce involved! This slow cooker recipe smothers chicken in a sauce similar to a broccoli and cheese soup (without using any canned condensed soup, might I add), with the broccoli breaking up and mixing right into the sauce as it cooks. Serve alongside my Quinoa Pilaf, recipe page: 175, for a complete meal that the complete family will love!

Shopping List

1 tablespoon **trans-fat free margarine**

4-6 boneless, skinless chicken breasts

1 cup **chicken broth**

8 ounces **light cream cheese**

2 cups **frozen broccoli florets**

½ teaspoon **salt**

¼ teaspoon **garlic powder**

1 cup shredded **sharp Cheddar cheese**

1. Add margarine to a large skillet over medium-high to high heat, until sizzling. Add chicken breasts and brown well, about 3 minutes each side.

2. Transfer chicken to a slow cooker set to low. Add the chicken broth to the skillet the chicken was cooked in over medium-high heat and use a spatula to scrape the bottom, breaking up any glaze the chicken may have left in the pan. Heat broth until simmering.

3. Add the cream cheese, broccoli florets, salt, and garlic powder to the slow cooker and then pour simmering chicken broth over top all.

4. Cover and let cook 5-6 hours, or until chicken is thoroughly cooked. After the first hour of cooking, stir well to disperse the cream cheese throughout.

5. When chicken is finished cooking, set the slow cooker to high and stir in shredded Cheddar cheese, until melted. Serve immediately.

George's Tips | If you are planning on leaving the house, you can skip the stirring an hour into cooking by melting the cream cheese in the skillet before adding the chicken broth in step 2.

Variation | The broccoli will break up into the sauce, and that's not a bad thing, but if you'd like something with a little more texture, start with fresh broccoli or (even better) cauliflower florets. Also, you can add 2 teaspoons of Dijon mustard for a little more zing.

Slow and Simple Pot Roast

calories: 450 | fat: 15g | protein: 65g | fiber: 0g | NET CARBS: **2g**

The trick to a good slow cooker pot roast is to not overload the cooker with too much added liquid. The 1¼ cups of beef broth in this recipe is all you need to get it done, as the meat itself will release quite a lot of juices as it cooks, and no liquid that you add will be as beefy as the meat's own juices!

1. Add olive oil to a large skillet over medium-high to high heat until almost smoking.

2. Season roast well with the salt, pepper, garlic powder, and Italian seasoning and place in skillet to brown. Sear each side for 4-5 minutes until well browned.

Shopping List

1 tablespoon **olive oil**
2-4 pound **boneless chuck roast**
1 teaspoon **salt**
½ teaspoon **black pepper**
¼ teaspoon **garlic powder**
½ teaspoon **Italian seasoning**
1¼ cups **beef broth**
1 **yellow onion**, chopped
1 **bay leaf**

3. Transfer roast to a slow cooker set on the lowest setting. Pour beef broth into the large skillet, scraping any browned bits off the bottom. Pour broth and juices from the skillet over the roast in slow cooker.

4. Cover roast with the chopped onion, and place a bay leaf in the liquid at the bottom of the cooker. Cover and let cook 8-10 hours, whenever you are ready to serve.

George's Tips | I like to cook my vegetables separately from the roast, but you can add some sections of celery, sliced mushrooms, and thick sliced zucchini or yellow squash in the last hour and a half of cooking.

Variation | Make a quick and easy gravy by spooning out about 1½ cups of the liquid from the cooker after cooking (try to get all the darkest liquid with the most beef bits in it from the bottom of the cooker, not just the fat off the top) and transferring to a sauce pot on the stove. Add 1 tablespoon of trans-fat free margarine and ¼ cup of heavy cream, and simmer over medium-high heat until the liquid reduces and is thick enough to lightly coat the back of a spoon.

Slow Cooker

Crantastic Cranberry Meatballs

calories: 310 | fat: 15g | protein: 34g | fiber: 2g | NET CARBS: 7g

This is a really good party or holiday recipe that your guests would never know is low in carbs. Just leave it in the slow cooker and let it stay warm for as long as the night goes on. The ground turkey meatballs in cranberry sauce may remind you of a certain holiday, but that doesn't mean you can't serve it year round!

Shopping List

MEATBALLS

2 pounds **ground turkey**
2 large **eggs**
¼ cup finely minced **onion**
½ teaspoon **salt**

SAUCE

12 ounces **cranberries**, fresh or frozen
2 cups **beef broth**
1 cup **bulk sugar substitute**
2 tablespoons **tomato paste**

1. Prepare the meatballs by combining the ground turkey, eggs, minced onion, and salt in a large mixing bowl. Use your hands to mix well.

2. Combine all sauce ingredients in a slow cooker and set to high until simmering.

3. Using your hands, form turkey mixture into golf ball sized meatballs, dropping them into the slow cooker as you go. When all meatballs are in, cover slow cooker and reduce heat to low.

4. Let cook at least 4 hours before serving, though they're even better after 6 hours!

George's Tips | Garnish with a sprinkle of fresh orange zest to add a little color and a whole different flavor!

Variation | For a spicier take on these, try adding 2 teaspoons chili powder, and 2 teaspoons of Worcestershire sauce to the slow cooker in step 2.

Ground Sirloin Chili

calories: 305 | fat: 14g | protein: 36g | fiber: 2g | NET CARBS: **5g**

This slow cooker chili recipe is about as easy as it gets, making a real meaty, thick chili that is bean free (follow the variation if that last statement disappointed you!). Ground sirloin is not only delicious but extremely lean. With so much less fat, the meat could easily get dry and tough in other dishes, but when you're slow cooking all day that isn't going to be an issue!

Shopping List

1 tablespoon **olive oil**

2 pounds **ground sirloin**

1 **yellow onion**, chopped

1 can (**14-16** ounces) **diced tomatoes**

1 can (**8** ounces) **tomato sauce**

1 **green bell pepper**, chopped

2 tablespoons **chili powder**

1¼ teaspoons **salt**

½ teaspoon **black pepper**

1. Add olive oil and ground sirloin to a large skillet over medium-high to high heat, browning well, about 6 minutes.

2. When meat is almost browned, drain off any excess fat, return to heat, and add onions to cook just until they sweat. Transfer all to a slow cooker set to low.

3. Add can of diced tomatoes (including the juice) and all remaining ingredients to the slow cooker and stir all to combine.

4. Cover and let cook 5-9 hours, whenever you are ready to serve.

George's Tips | I only make my chili with ground sirloin when it goes on sale, so it should be said that any kind of ground beef can be used in place of the ground sirloin if you wish. I also like to add ¼ teaspoon of cayenne pepper and ½ teaspoon of ground cumin to make it spicy!

Variation | Make a "black bean" chili by adding 1 drained can of black soy beans, usually found in the organic foods section of the grocery store. For a few more carbohydrates, you can add a can of regular black beans instead. Top with shredded Cheddar jack cheese and a dollop of sour cream.

Teriyaki Chicken Thighs

calories: 225 | fat: 10g | protein: 28.5g | fiber: 0g | NET CARBS: **4g**

With all of the dishes we've come up with, I don't know of any single dish that we've made as many times as Teriyaki Chicken Thighs. They're inexpensive, easy, and delicious, so it seemed only fitting to make them even easier for this book. By cooking them all day, there's no need to marinate beforehand!

Shopping List

2 tablespoons **sesame oil**

8-12 boneless, skinless chicken thighs

½ cup **teriyaki sauce**

2 rounded teaspoons **minced garlic**

1 tablespoon **bulk sugar substitute**

1. Add sesame oil to a large skillet over medium-high to high heat, until almost smoking. Add chicken thighs and brown well, about 3 minutes each side.

2. Transfer chicken and any oil from the pan to a slow cooker set to low.

3. Add the teriyaki sauce, minced garlic, sugar substitute, and ¼ cup of tap water to the slow cooker.

4. Cover and let cook 6-8 hours, or until you are ready to serve. Use tongs to remove from liquid in cooker and serve garnished with toasted sesame seeds, if you desire.

George's Tips | If you can, it's best to stir this at least once halfway through cooking, so the thighs on the top can get to the bottom and into the sauce. The teriyaki sauce in this recipe refers to regular sauce, not "teriyaki marinade" which would contain a lot of added sugar.

Variation | Low sodium teriyaki sauce can be used in place of the regular to cut down on the sodium content. 2-3 teaspoons of orange zest can be added to make Teriyaki Orange Chicken Thighs.

Slow Cooker

Creamy Chicken and Sweet Potato Stew

Creamy Chicken and Sweet Potato Stew

calories: 255 | fat: 8.5g | protein: 31g | fiber: 1.5g | NET CARBS: 9g

While chicken and sweet potatoes may not sound like a perfect pair, I can tell you that they are perfectly matched in this creamy stew that kind of reminds me of the inside of a pot pie. The sweet potatoes add that slight hint of sweetness that carrots would in a pot pie, but with a whole lot more flavor.

Shopping List

1½ pounds **chicken breasts**
1 tablespoon **olive oil**
½ cup chopped **onion**
5 cups **chicken broth**
2 **sweet potatoes**, peeled
1 teaspoon **poultry seasoning**
½ cup **heavy cream**
salt and **pepper**

1. Cut chicken into 1 inch cubes. Add olive oil and chicken to a large skillet over medium-high to high heat, browning well, about 4 minutes each side. When meat is almost browned, add onions to cook just until they sweat.

2. Transfer chicken and onions to a slow cooker set to low. Add some of the chicken broth to the skillet the chicken was cooked in, and use a spatula to scrape the bottom, breaking up any glaze the chicken may have left in the pan. Pour over chicken and onions in slow cooker, and then pour in remaining chicken broth.

3. Cut sweet potatoes into ½ inch cubes and add to the cooker, along with poultry seasoning. Stir all.

4. Cover and let cook 6-8 hours, depending on when you are ready to serve. Stir in the heavy cream and salt and pepper to taste. Thicken the stew before serving by mashing a few of the cooked sweet potato cubes into the broth.

George's Tips | I like to serve garnished with a (very) small pinch of ground cinnamon.

Variation | If sweet potatoes and chicken doesn't sound like a winning combination to you, try skipping the potatoes and mixing in a finished batch of Quinoa Pilaf, recipe page: 175, before serving to make a whole grain take on a Chicken and "Rice" soup.

Slow Cooker

Eat as the Romans Do Beef Stew

calories: 345 | fat: 14.5g | protein: 40g | fiber: 2g | NET CARBS: **5g**

I like to serve this hearty, tomato rich beef stew over steamed cauliflower. Though I haven't exactly seen any depictions of ancient Romans eating bowls of cauliflower, it's good, and I'm sure you will agree. If you are of Roman descent and you agree, let me know that my recipe title is valid!

1. Add olive oil and beef to a large skillet over medium-high to high heat, browning well, about 4 minutes each side. When meat is almost completely browned, add onions to cook just until they sweat.

2. Transfer beef and onions to a slow cooker set to low. Add the beef broth to the skillet the beef was cooked in and use a spatula to scrape the bottom, breaking up any glaze the beef may have left in the pan. Pour over beef and onions in slow cooker.

Shopping List

1 tablespoon **olive oil**
2 pounds **beef stewing meat**, cubed
½ **red onion**, sliced thick
1½ cups **beef broth**
1 can (**14-16** ounces) **diced tomatoes**
2 teaspoons fresh chopped **basil**
3 tablespoons **tomato paste**
¼ teaspoon **garlic powder**
8 ounces **mushrooms**, halved
¼ cup grated **Parmesan cheese**

Slow Cooker

3. Add diced tomatoes, tomato paste, basil, and garlic powder to the slow cooker and stir all to combine. Place mushrooms over top, lightly pressing down with a spoon to submerge, while still keeping them at the top of the cooker.

4. Cover and let cook 4-6 hours, or until meat is tender. Stir in Parmesan cheese (and depending on the beef broth used, you may want to salt to taste) before serving.

George's Tips | ¾ of a teaspoon of Italian seasoning can be substituted for the fresh basil in this recipe if you don't have any fresh herbs on hand.

Variation | Skip the Parmesan cheese, and stir in ¼ cup of burgundy wine and ½ cup of heavy cream before serving for a slow cooker dish similar to Steak Diane.

prep time 10 mins	cook time 6+ hrs	serving 3 ribs	serves 4-8

Sweet and Sour Spareribs

calories: 530 | fat: 38g | protein: 40g | fiber: 1g | NET CARBS: **3g**

This recipe for Sweet and Sour Spareribs makes a nice and thick sauce that is tomato based, rather than the traditionally sugar based sauce (I'm looking at YOU Chinese restaurants). Don't worry, all the sweet flavor is still there, as well as the sour that the name implies. Just don't forget the secret and positively pivotal ingredient—green bell pepper!

Shopping List

2-4 pounds **spareribs**
¼ cup finely diced **green bell pepper**
1 cup **bulk sugar substitute**
3 tablespoons **tomato paste**
1 cup **tomato sauce**
⅓ cup **white vinegar**
2 tablespoons **soy sauce**

1. Cut spareribs into sections of 3 ribs each to better fit into the slow cooker.

2. Place all remaining ingredients in a slow cooker set to low and stir to combine. Add the spareribs a few sections at a time, using a pair of tongs to bring the pieces from the bottom to the top to evenly coat all with the sauce.

3. Cover and let cook on low for 8-10 hours, or set the cooker to high and cook 4-6 hours, until meat is tender and to your liking.

George's Tips | For even better ribs, brown in an oiled skillet over high heat before adding to the slow cooker. For even better ribs than that, grill 2-3 minutes on each side before slow cooking to lock in that grilled flavor!

Variation | If you are not watching your sugar intake, 3-4 tablespoons of honey can be used in place of the sugar substitute to keep things all natural. Meatballs can also be cooked in this sauce as long as you reduce the cooking time to 4-6 hours on low.

Slow Cooker

Vegetables and Sides

Sides

| Cheesy Yellow Squash Casserole

Cheesy Yellow Squash Casserole

calories: 160 | fat: 12g | protein: 7.5g | fiber: 1.5g | NET CARBS: 5g

Yellow squash casserole is one of those family recipe classics that a lot of people make without even realizing it is naturally low in carbohydrates. I've taken that a step further by eliminating the high carb breadcrumb toppings that most recipes call for, and utilized reduced fat cream cheese to cut down on the fat.

Shopping List

nonstick cooking spray

1½ pounds **yellow squash**, thinly sliced into discs

salt and **pepper**

¼ cup diced **yellow onion**

¼ cup diced **red bell pepper**

8 ounces **reduced fat cream cheese**

½ cup shredded **sharp Cheddar cheese**

1. Preheat the oven to 375 degrees. Spray a 2 quart baking dish with nonstick cooking spray.

2. Layer the bottom of the baking dish with half of the yellow squash slices and lightly sprinkle with salt and pepper. Top with ½ of the onions, ½ of the red bell pepper, dollops of ½ of the cream cheese, and then ½ of the Cheddar cheese over top.

3. Repeat the process of step 2 all over again, creating a second layer of yellow squash and then the other ingredients, ending with the remaining Cheddar cheese on top.

4. Bake for 40-45 minutes or until the top is beginning to brown and squash is fork tender. Let rest 5 minutes before serving.

George's Tips | Cut down on the cooking time by lightly boiling, steaming, or sautéing the yellow squash before baking until nearly tender. Simply bake until cheese is melted.

Variation | You can also make this with the strands of one cooked spaghetti squash in place of the yellow squash. See the first two steps of Spaghetti Squash with Ricotta Blush Sauce, recipe page: 147, for directions on how to prepare a spaghetti squash.

Sides

It's a Snap Peas

calories: 65 | fat: 2.5g | protein: 3g | fiber: 3g | NET CARBS: **5.5g**

Sugar snap peas are an often overlooked vegetable, usually kept amongst tons of other vegetables in the occasional stir fry, but they're an amazing side all by their lonesome! This recipe couldn't be any easier, and keeps the natural flavor of the snap peas out in front, where it rightfully should be.

Shopping List

1 pound **sugar snap peas**
1 tablespoon **trans-fat free margarine**
1 teaspoon **lemon zest**
½ teaspoon **salt**
¼ teaspoon **black pepper**

1. Bring a large pot of water to a boil over high heat. Add snap peas and boil for only 1-2 minutes, just until crisp-tender.

2. Transfer snap peas to a colander to drain. Return empty pot to the stove and turn off heat. Add margarine to the pot and let it melt from the residual heat.

3. Cover melted margarine with the drained snap peas, lemon zest, salt, and pepper. Toss all to combine and serve hot.

George's Tips | Though a lot of people like to snap off the ends and remove the fiber that runs the lenth of the snap peas, I don't find it very necessary. The ends of snap peas aren't nearly as tough as green beans and cook up quite soft. So save some time and eat them whole!

Variation | Add a teaspoon of chopped fresh mint in step 3 to bring another great flavor to the snap peas. Or simply garnish with fresh mint.

Roasted Brussels Sprouts

calories: 95 | fat: 5g | protein: 4g | fiber: 4.5g | NET CARBS: **6g**

Now, I realize that putting a Brussels sprouts recipe in this book may not be a good idea, but I've been avoiding them for far too long! (And only because other people don't like them, as I love them!) While I may not be able to convert everyone into loving them, this recipe roasts the Brussels sprouts until they're crispy, delicious, and almost nutty in flavor.

Shopping List

1 pound **Brussels sprouts**
1½ tablespoons **olive oil**
1 tablespoon **minced garlic**
½ teaspoon **salt**
¼ teaspoon **black pepper**

1. Place oven rack in the center position and preheat to 425 degrees.

2. Slice Brussels sprouts in half lengthwise and add to a large bowl. Cover with remaining ingredients and toss all to coat.

3. Place the coated Brussels sprouts on a sheet pan and bake for 15-20 minutes, shaking the pan to mix them up halfway through. When finished they should be crispy and very brown on the outside and tender on the inside. Serve immediately as they will lose a lot of their crispness as they sit.

George's Tips | I like to give these another small sprinkling of salt as soon as I take them out of the oven.

Variation | Add a tablespoon of balsamic vinegar to the bowl in step 2 for a stronger flavor. You can also eat them like a warm salad, drizzled in Italian vinaigrette after baking.

Sides

Grilled Sweet Potato Planks

calories: 85 | fat: 3g | protein: 1g | fiber: 2g | NET CARBS: **11g**

I'm not a very big fan of traditional baked sweet potatoes, so I didn't know what to do when Rachel started growing them in our backyard! Thankfully, I got this idea to cut them into planks and grill them one day, and I've got to say—these things are good. Like sweet and salty potato wedges, this is just one of those recipes that is more than the sum of its parts.

Shopping List

2 **sweet potatoes**
1 tablespoon **olive oil**
salt

1. Oil and then light or preheat a grill to medium-high to high.

2. Clean sweet potatoes under running water and then slice in half lengthwise. Slice each half into 3 wedges for a small potato, or 5-6 wedges for a large.

3. Spread sweet potato planks out on a sheet pan and drizzle all with olive oil, tossing to coat. Once coated, sprinkle liberally with salt.

4. Grill planks perpendicular to the grill's grates so they do not fall through. Grill 8-10 minutes, turning every few minutes, until they are tender on the inside. If you are unsure if they are done, the best way to test is to remove one from the grill and press it with your finger to feel for softness.

George's Tips | A coarse salt like kosher salt works best on these, a lot like a salted soft pretzel. If you don't like too much char on your grilled foods, you can also pre-boil the cut sweet potato planks before grilling to get the cooking process started, but I don't find that necessary.

Variation | Sprinkle the finished, grilled planks with bulk sugar substitute and a very light amount of ground cinnamon to make these into an amazing grilled dessert! (I'd still use the salt in step 3, as I love sweet and salty desserts!)

Sides

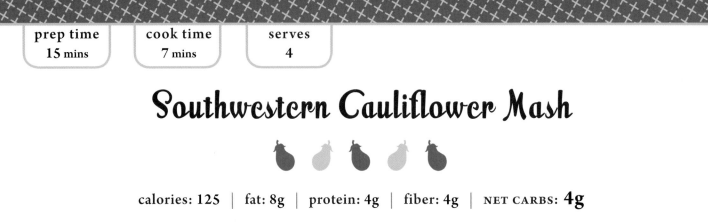

prep time	cook time	serves
15 mins	7 mins	4

Southwestern Cauliflower Mash

calories: 125 | fat: 8g | protein: 4g | fiber: 4g | NET CARBS: **4g**

I can still remember the first time I pureed or "mashed" cauliflower and my whole family looked at me like I was losing it! Now, just a few years later, pureed cauliflower is in restaurants (and some of the nicest too!) all over the country, especially alongside or under steaks. While I may not be able to call it unique anymore, this southwestern version is definitely new.

Shopping List

1 medium head **cauliflower**

2 tablespoons **trans-fat free margarine**, softened

½ cup **light sour cream**

⅛ teaspoon **garlic powder**

1 can (4 ounces) **diced mild green chilies**, drained

salt and **pepper**

1. Bring a large pot of water to a boil over high heat.

2. Clean and cut cauliflower into small florets and pieces. Cook florets and pieces in boiling water for about 6 minutes, or until very tender.

3. Drain well. Carefully pat the cooked cauliflower dry between several layers of paper towels.

4. With a handheld blender in a deep bowl or using a food processor, pulse the cooked cauliflower with the margarine, sour cream, and garlic powder. Pulse all until almost entirely smooth.

5. Stir in green chilies and then salt and pepper to taste. Microwave 30-45 seconds to serve steaming hot. Garnish with fresh cilantro, if desired.

George's Tips | For even more flavor, I like to add 4-5 roasted garlic cloves to the puree in step 4. Simply spread out and roast the cloves on a sheet pan in a 400 degree oven for about 15 minutes, or until they are brown and very aromatic. Squeeze them out of their peels and into the bowl with cauliflower before pureeing.

Variation | You can substitute chunky salsa in place of the green chilies, but I would use a fine mesh strainer to strain off most of the liquid, adding 3-4 tablespoons of just the chunky stuff!

Spaghetti Squash with Ricotta Blush Sauce

calories: 115 | fat: 6g | protein: 9g | fiber: 1g | NET CARBS: **5g**

Spaghetti squash is a pretty amazing thing, but after taking the time to prepare one you don't always want to take too much time preparing a dish out of it! This recipe consolidates your time, allowing you to make a creamy ricotta and tomato sauce from scratch before the spaghetti squash is even done cooking!

1. Bring a large pot of water to a boil over high heat. Slice spaghetti squash in half lengthwise and scoop out the seeds with a spoon as you would a pumpkin.

2. Completely submerge squash halves in the pot of boiling water and cook for about 20 minutes, or until the inside is just tender to a fork and pulls apart in strands.

Shopping List

1 medium **spaghetti squash**
1½ cups **part skim ricotta cheese**
½ cup **tomato sauce**
2 rounded teaspoons **minced garlic**
2 rounded teaspoons fresh chopped **basil**
¼ cup grated **Parmesan cheese**
salt and **pepper**

3. As the squash is cooking, place a sauce pot over medium heat and add the ricotta cheese, tomato sauce, minced garlic, and basil. Bring up to a simmer, stirring frequently. Add the Parmesan cheese and then salt and pepper to taste. Turn heat to low until ready to serve, stirring occasionally.

4. Once the spaghetti squash is cooked, drain and run under warm water, just until the temperature has lowered enough to handle it. Use a large spoon to scoop the flesh from the squash in large chunks, then a fork to separate the chunks into spaghetti like strands. (It is best to do this into your serving dish.)

5. Serve squash topped with the ricotta sauce, hot off the stove.

George's Tips | It is better to undercook the spaghetti squash than overcook it. If the squash is a little crunchy or "al dente" (or if it has cooled down too much for the sauce to heat back up), transfer the strands (after step 4) to a microwave safe dish, add a few tablespoons of water, cover, and microwave in 1 minute increments until hot and crisp-tender.

Variation | Add 2 tablespoons trans-fat free margarine, 1 fresh chopped tomato, and ¼ cup of crumbled bacon in step 3 to make an even richer, chunkier sauce.

Sides

| Tomato and Feta Stuffed Eggplants

Tomato and Feta Stuffed Eggplants

calories: 180 | fat: 11g | protein: 6g | fiber: 10g | NET CARBS: 9g

These Tomato and Feta Stuffed Eggplants are the perfect all-in-one side dish to any simple or grilled meat dish. If your local grocery store sells baby eggplants, you can even make this recipe with 4 baby eggplants, cut in half, making 8 party appetizers!

1. Preheat the oven to 350 degrees. Slice tops off eggplant, and discard. Slice eggplants in half lengthwise, and use a pointed spoon to scoop out the pulp in as large of chunks as possible. Scoop until eggplant skins are only about ½ inch thick.

2. Add olive oil to a nonstick skillet over medium-high heat. Roughly chop the removed eggplant pulp and add to the pan. Add the garlic and sauté for 2-3 minutes.

Shopping List

2 small **eggplants** or **1** large
2 tablespoons **olive oil**
2 teaspoons **minced garlic**
2 tomatoes, chopped
½ teaspoon dry **oregano**, or 1½ teaspoons fresh chopped
¼ teaspoon **salt**
¼ teaspoon **black pepper**
½ cup **feta cheese**

3. Remove pan from heat, and add the tomatoes, oregano, salt, and pepper to the eggplant sauté. Mix all to combine and make the filling.

4. Place eggplant shells on a baking sheet and stuff each with an even amount of the filling. Top all with the feta cheese, and loosely cover with tin foil. Bake for 30 minutes or until the eggplant skin is soft. Serve drizzled with additional olive oil, and garnished with fresh oregano.

George's Tips | Try oiling and grilling the bottom of the eggplant shells for 3 minutes before stuffing, and reducing the baking time to 20 minutes, for even more flavor.

Variation | Start step 2 by browning ½ pound of lean ground beef, and add a pinch more of the seasonings to make great Beef, Tomato, and Feta Stuffed Eggplants. You may have a little extra filling leftover, so grab a fork!

Lemon and Garlic Broccoli Florets

calories: 80 | fat: 4g | protein: 4.5g | fiber: 4g | NET CARBS: **6g**

This simple, yet effective way of preparing broccoli is an old standard that I've been cooking as long as I've been a chef. When it comes to green vegetables and when in doubt, toss in some lemon and garlic! Make it up any day of the week as this is about as easy as it gets!

Shopping List

1 bunch **broccoli**

1½ tablespoons **trans-fat free margarine**

2 rounded teaspoons **minced garlic**

2 teaspoons **lemon zest**

½ teaspoon **salt**

⅛ teaspoon **black pepper**

1. Rinse broccoli well and then cut florets from the large stem leaving their smaller stems intact. Discard large stem or slice the top portion of it into discs to cook with the florets.

2. Bring a large pot of water to a boil over high heat. Add broccoli florets to water and boil 4-6 minutes until bright green and crisp-tender. You can also use a steamer over the water, if you have one.

3. Transfer broccoli to a colander to drain. Return pot to the stove and heat margarine over medium-high heat until sizzling.

4. Add minced garlic and lemon zest to the sizzling margarine and then cover with drained broccoli. Sprinkle with the salt and pepper and stir to combine. Remove from heat and serve.

George's Tips | You can make this straight from a bag of frozen broccoli florets by starting at step 3 and sautéing 6-8 minutes until florets are heated through.

Variation | Make Asian inspired Orange Broccoli by replacing the lemon zest with orange zest, adding 2 teaspoons of sesame oil in step 3 (along with the margarine), and substituting 1 tablespoon of low-sodium soy sauce in place of the salt.

Sides

Gorgonzola Coleslaw

calories: 98 | fat: 7g | protein: 4g | fiber: 2g | NET CARBS: **4.5g**

This recipe for coleslaw is a little sweet, but a lot of savory thanks to a homemade chunky gorgonzola (a type of bleu cheese) coleslaw dressing prepared in only five minutes. Serve it alongside a grilled steak as a refreshing change and you won't have to prepare a salad or a side dish! Or simply serve it before the meal *as* the salad.

Shopping List

1 bag (**16** ounces) **shredded coleslaw cabbage**
2 tablespoons **cider vinegar**
½ cup **light sour cream**
⅓ cup **light mayonnaise**
⅓ cup **crumbled gorgonzola (bleu) cheese**
1 tablespoon **bulk sugar substitute**
¾ teaspoon **salt**
⅛ teaspoon **black pepper**

1. Add all ingredients to a large bowl, tossing to combine. The mixture may seem thick at first, but the cabbage will release some of its water into the dressing as it chills.

2. Cover and refrigerate for at least 1 hour to let the flavors mingle before serving. Serve topped with additional gorgonzola cheese crumbles.

George's Tips | Any bleu cheese will work fine for this recipe, but gorgonzola tends to be creamier and mixes into the slaw really well. White wine vinegar can also be used in place of the cider vinegar if that is all you have in your pantry. You can also substitute a bag of broccoli slaw mix in place of the coleslaw mix, though they usually contain carrots which are high in natural sugars.

Variation | Add any of these delicious ingredients, or make it fully loaded by adding all: ½ cup of peeled and chopped apple, 2 tablespoons of diced red onion, 2 tablespoons of diced celery, or ¼ cup of chopped walnuts. Sprinkling crumbled bacon over top wouldn't hurt either!

Sides

Thick Cut Cauliflower "Steaks" with Balsamic Drizzle

prep time	cook time	yield	serves
10 mins	18 mins	2 "steaks"	2

Thick Cut Cauliflower "Steaks" with Balsamic Drizzle

calories: 220 | fat: 12g | protein: 9g | fiber: 10.5g | NET CARBS: **12g**

These cauliflower "steaks" are a surprisingly hearty side dish, considering it comes from something as light as cauliflower! Serve them alongside a real steak and make a double batch of the balsamic sauce to drizzle over both.

1. Preheat the oven to 300 degrees. Slice sides that do not go all the way down to the stalk off of the entire head of cauliflower. Save for salads, dipping, or another meal. Slice remaining center of cauliflower into two thick "steaks".

2. Add half of the vegetable oil to a skillet over medium-high heat. Season "steaks" with a pinch of salt and pepper and add one to the skillet to brown. Brown on both sides, 2-3 minutes. Transfer to a baking pan, and repeat browning with the second "steak" using remaining vegetable oil.

3. Once both "steaks" are browned, and on the baking pan, bake for 12 minutes, or until as tender as you would like it.

4. While the "steaks" are baking, prepare the sauce by adding margarine, soy sauce, balsamic vinegar, and sugar substitute to a small sauce pan over medium-high heat, and heating until simmering. Remove from heat.

5. Serve "steaks" drizzled with the balsamic sauce.

Shopping List

1 large head **cauliflower**
1 tablespoon **vegetable oil**
salt and **pepper**
1 tablespoon **trans-fat free margarine**
1 tablespoon **low-sodium soy sauce**
2 teaspoons **balsamic vinegar**
1 teaspoon **bulk sugar substitute**, optional

George's Tips | Slicing the cauliflower can be tricky. The best way to do it is to use a very large knife, cutting one of the sides off first, and then cut the two steaks off, using the other side to hold in place. Keep your fingers bent and entirely out of the way of the knife!

Variation | You can make the unused sides of the head of cauliflower in this way as well for more portions, though as they are not connected to the stalk, they may not hold together as well. They may also require a few more minutes baking, as they will most likely be thicker than the "steaks".

Sides

Zucchini and Tomato Gratin

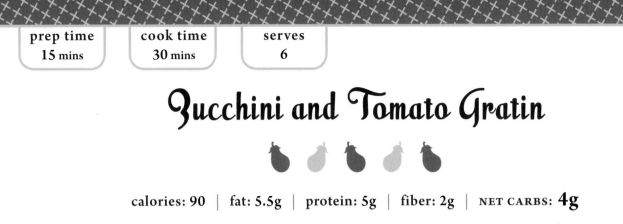

calories: 90 | fat: 5.5g | protein: 5g | fiber: 2g | NET CARBS: **4g**

While this casserole has Italian flavors, it uses a French technique for a nice and crunchy Parmesan cheese topping. Thankfully, it only sounds complicated to make a gratin—in reality, it's about as easy as it gets.

Shopping List

3 medium **zucchini**
2 large **tomatoes**
salt and **pepper**
½ cup + **2** tablespoons grated **Parmesan cheese**
1½ teaspoons **Italian seasoning**
1 tablespoon **minced garlic**
1 tablespoon **olive oil**

1. Preheat the oven to 400 degrees. Cut ends off zucchini and tomatoes and discard. Slice zucchini and tomatoes into thin discs.

2. Layer the bottom of an 8 inch baking dish with half of the zucchini slices. Lightly sprinkle with salt, pepper, 1 tablespoon of the Parmesan cheese, and ½ teaspoon of Italian seasoning.

3. Layer all tomato slices atop zucchini in baking dish. Again, lightly sprinkle with salt, pepper, 1 tablespoon of the Parmesan cheese, and ½ teaspoon of Italian seasoning.

4. Repeat one last time by adding the remaining zucchini on top of the tomatoes. Lightly sprinkle with salt, pepper, the remaining ½ teaspoon of Italian seasoning, and the remaining ½ cup of Parmesan cheese on top.

5. Bake for about 25-30 minutes or until the top is well browned and zucchini is fork tender.

George's Tips | The top should be nice and brown, but if it looks to be getting too brown for your taste, simply cover with aluminum foil and continue baking. Zucchini and tomatoes release a lot of water once cooked, so be sure to serve with a slotted spatula, to allow gratin to drain.

Variation | Yellow squash can be used in place, or along with the zucchini. You can also use fresh herbs for even better results. I like to use about 12 fresh basil leaves atop the tomato layer and a sprinkling of fresh chopped oregano on the top layer.

Sides

Green Beans with One Slice of Bacon

calories: 90 | fat: 5g | protein: 4g | fiber: 4g | NET CARBS: **4.5g**

This recipe may seem a little strange, but let me tell you that one singular slice of bacon can dress up a bag of frozen green beans like nothing else! While combining green beans with bacon is nothing new, (the bacon here is used more as a seasoning than an ingredient) this version keeps things surprisingly low in fat but full of flavor. Just don't use two slices of bacon or I'll have to rename the recipe!

1. Place bacon in a large nonstick skillet over medium-high heat and cook 4-5 minutes, flipping once, until most of the fat has cooked out and into the pan.

Shopping List

1 slice **raw bacon**

1 bag (**14-16** ounces) **frozen whole green beans**

1 tablespoon **trans-fat free margarine**

2 tablespoons finely diced **red onion**

¼ teaspoon **salt**

⅛ teaspoon **black pepper**

2. Add frozen green beans, margarine, diced red onion, salt, and pepper and stir all to combine.

3. Cover and cook 4-6 minutes, uncovering and stirring every minute, just until green beans have heated all the way through.

4. Break up, or simply eat, or do whatever you wish with the one slice of bacon and serve the green beans immediately.

George's Tips | Of course you can also make this with fresh green beans, but you should boil them for about 8 minutes beforehand to get them almost tender before sautéing.

Variation | You can use a tablespoon of diced shallots, or a teaspoon of minced garlic (or both!) in place of the diced red onion. Or if all you've got is what's in your pantry—simply add a pinch of garlic powder!

Sides

Japanese Zucchini Stir Fry

calories: 75 | fat: 5g | protein: 2g | fiber: 1.5g | NET CARBS: **4g**

I used to love eating in Japanese steakhouses where they cook right at the table, but realized that two thirds of what they give you is starchy rice and noodles. That's when I started cooking the good stuff at home, like this Japanese Zucchini Stir Fry. Just make sure to serve alongside some Whole Wheat Lo Mein, recipe page: 172, and with the white sauce recipe in the variation below.

Shopping List

2 medium **zucchini**
1 **yellow onion**, peeled and quartered
1 tablespoon **trans-fat free margarine**
2 teaspoons **sesame oil**
2 tablespoons **soy sauce**
¼ teaspoon **black pepper**

1. Slice ends off zucchini and discard. Cut each zucchini in half crosswise and then each half in half again lengthwise. Slice these quarters of the zucchini into thick sticks. Cut quartered onion into ¼ thick strips.

2. Cook margarine and sesame oil in a sauté pan or wok over medium-high heat until sizzling. Add zucchini and onions, and cook without stirring for 2-4 minutes, until they begin to brown. Stir once and continue cooking another 2-3 minutes to brown them further.

3. Add soy sauce and black pepper to stir fry and stir all to combine. Remove from heat and serve garnished with toasted sesame seeds, if you desire.

George's Tips | To make toasted sesame seeds for the garnish, simply heat sesame seeds in an ungreased skillet over medium heat for 3-5 minutes, or until they turn a nice brown.

Variation | Make a Japanese White Sauce to dip the stir fry into by combining ½ cup mayonnaise, 1 tablespoon melted trans-fat free margarine, 1 teaspoon tomato paste, ¼ teaspoon garlic powder, and ⅛ teaspoon paprika.

Sides

Awesome Grilled Asparagus

calories: 80 | fat: 7g | protein: 3g | fiber: 2.5g | NET CARBS: **2g**

The great thing about grilling vegetables as opposed to boiling them is that you keep a lot more of their natural nutrients intact. If you've ever turned a pot of water green by boiling asparagus, you can see what I'm saying. Asparagus are one of my favorite vegetables to grill, as they stay nice and crisp, and take on a lot of that good grilled flavor without overpowering their own natural flavors.

Shopping List

1 pound **asparagus**
2 tablespoons **olive oil**
2 rounded teaspoons **minced garlic**
¼ teaspoon **salt**
¼ teaspoon **black pepper**

1. Oil and then light or preheat a grill to medium-high to high.

2. Trim the hard ends of the stalk off of the asparagus, about 1½ to 2 inches up from the bottom. Discard.

3. Spread trimmed asparagus out on a sheet pan and drizzle all with olive oil. Cover with the minced garlic, salt, and pepper and toss to coat.

4. Grill asparagus huddled close together, perpendicular to the grill's grates so they do not fall through. Grill about 4 minutes, turning them in large groups with tongs twice. Serve alongside grilled meat.

George's Tips | I like to buy pencil thin asparagus, but if your asparagus is very thick you may have to grill an additional 2-3 minutes to get them as tender as you want them.

Variation | Try squeezing a few teaspoons of fresh lemon juice over the asparagus in step 3 to give them a little bit of a bite.

Sides

prep time 15 mins	cook time 20 mins	serves 8

The Original Cauliflower "Mac" and Cheese

calories: 180 | fat: 13g | protein: 7g | fiber: 3g | NET CARBS: **4g**

This recipe for a pasta-free baked "macaroni" and cheese casserole is not only an all time favorite of my family, but also one of the top rated casserole recipes of all time on Food Network's website. The Dijon mustard was a last minute suggestion by one of the staff on my television show, literally seconds before the cameras started rolling! She was right—it adds just the right amount of zing to this Stella Style classic.

Shopping List

nonstick cooking spray

1 large head **cauliflower**, cut into small florets

¾ cup **heavy cream**

2 ounces **light cream cheese**

1½ teaspoons **Dijon mustard**

2 cups shredded **sharp Cheddar cheese**

⅛ teaspoon **garlic powder**

¼ teaspoon **salt**

¼ teaspoon **black pepper**

1. Preheat oven to 375 degrees. Bring a large pot of water to a boil. Spray an 8x8 inch baking dish with vegetable oil spray.

2. Cook the cauliflower in the boiling water until crisp-tender, about 5 minutes.

3. Drain well and pat between several layers of paper towels to dry. Transfer the cauliflower to the baking dish and set aside.

4. Bring the cream to a simmer in a small saucepan over medium heat, and whisk in the cream cheese and mustard until smooth. Stir in 1 ½ cups of the Cheddar cheese and all of the garlic powder, salt and pepper. Whisk just until the cheese melts, 1 to 2 minutes.

5. Remove sauce from heat and pour over the cauliflower, stirring to combine. Top with the remaining ½ cup Cheddar cheese and bake until browned and bubbly hot, about 15 minutes.

George's Tips | 2 ounces is ¼ of a regular brick of cream cheese. For quicker melting, break the cream cheese into smaller pieces before stirring into the sauce.

Variation | Unsweetened soy milk can be used in place of the heavy cream to lighten up on the fat. Add in 1 cup of cubed ham (sold already cubed in most grocery stores, though I prefer leftover baked ham!) for a complete family meal!

Sides

Wholesome Whole Grains and Legumes

Whole Grain

Whole Wheat Penne Primavera

calories: 235 | fat: 6.5g | protein: 10g | fiber: 8g | NET CARBS: **30g**

Rachel loves making this recipe for lunch, as it is light and so abundant with vegetables (usually from her garden) that we can save the leftovers in the fridge for the next night's dinner. Grill up some chicken or Italian sausage for a complete, nutritious meal.

1. Bring a large pot of water to a boil, and cook penne according to directions on box. Drain and rinse with cold water to stop the cooking process. Set aside.

2. While the pasta is cooking, thinly slice zucchini into discs, discarding the ends. Next, thinly slice yellow bell pepper into strips.

3. Place a large nonstick pan over medium heat and add in olive oil, zucchini discs, and yellow pepper strips. Sauté 5-6 minutes or until vegetables are crisp-tender.

Shopping List

8 ounces **whole wheat penne**
2 medium **zucchini**
½ medium **yellow bell pepper**
2 tablespoons **olive oil**
2 teaspoons **minced garlic**
½ cup **vegetable broth**
1 teaspoon **Italian seasoning**
12 **grape tomatoes**, halved
salt and **pepper**
2 tablespoons grated **Parmesan cheese**

4. Add minced garlic, vegetable broth, and Italian seasoning, and bring up to a simmer. Once simmering, add the grape tomatoes and cooked penne pasta.

5. Cook an additional 2 minutes, stirring constantly, to heat the pasta throughout. Salt and pepper to taste and serve topped with the grated Parmesan cheese.

George's Tips | Freshly ground black pepper adds so much to this dish. Though I've suggested adding it to taste, I'd recommend at least ¼ of a teaspoon.

Variation | Add ½ cup of tomato sauce for a heartier dish. You can also substitute just about any vegetables for the ones in this recipe; asparagus, yellow squash, eggplant, mushrooms, onions… it's all good!

Whole Grain

Italian Sausage and Lentil Soup

calories: 230 | fat: 14g | protein: 14g | fiber: 4g | NET CARBS: **7g**

Italian sausage always makes a great soup, as tons of interesting flavors (especially fennel seed) are ground right into the meat. It also makes a perfect pair with the nutritious lentils in this recipe to leave you with a hearty soup that I could have almost called a stew!

Shopping List

1 tablespoon **olive oil**

½ pound **Italian sausages**, sliced into discs

½ cup chopped **yellow onion**

2 teaspoons **minced garlic**

⅓ cup **dry lentils**

4 cups **chicken broth**

1 can (**14-16** ounces) **diced tomatoes**

½ teaspoon **Italian seasoning**

1. Place olive oil and Italian sausage in a large pot over medium-high heat. Sauté 5-6 minutes or until sausage is well browned.

2. Add onions and garlic, and continue to sauté an additional 2 minutes.

3. Cover with remaining ingredients and stir all to combine. Bring up to a boil and then reduce heat to medium-low. Cover and let simmer for 35-40 minutes, or until lentils are tender. Remove from heat and serve!

George's Tips | Depending on the salt content of the chicken broth and Italian sausage used, you may need to salt to taste before serving. You can also skip the slicing of the Italian sausage links and buy loose ground Italian sausage near the ground beef, if your store carries it. You may also want to drain any excess grease after step 1 to reduce the fat in this recipe.

Variation | Add in 3 cups of fresh spinach leaves 2 minutes before serving and serve sprinkled with grated Parmesan cheese to make this soup even better!

Whole Grain

prep time	cook time	yield	serves
5 mins	4 mins ea.	8 pancakes	4

Whole Wheat Buttermilk Pancakes

calories: 225 | fat: 10g | protein: 9g | fiber: 4g | NET CARBS: 23g

Pancake batter is so amazingly easy to make that it's a wonder they sell so many varieties in a box! While nowadays you can even find whole wheat pancake mix in a box, it'll almost always be a mix of whole wheat and regular white flour, not 100% whole grain. Not to mention, powdered egg and buttermilk "solids" could never shake a stick at their real, fresh counterparts found here!

1. Combine buttermilk, eggs, sugar substitute, vegetable oil, baking powder, and salt in a large bowl and whisk until frothy.

2. Whisk whole wheat flour into the buttermilk mixture until batter is smooth and free of lumps.

Shopping List

1 cup **buttermilk**
2 large **eggs**
1 tablespoon **bulk sugar substitute**
2 tablespoons **vegetable oil**
2 teaspoons **baking powder**
½ teaspoon **salt**
1 cup **whole wheat flour**
nonstick cooking spray

3. Generously spray a nonstick pan or griddle with nonstick cooking spray and heat over medium heat.

4. Cook pancakes in batches, using about ¼ cup of batter per pancake. Cook until bubbles begin to form on the top, about 2 minutes, and then flip to cook an additional 2 minutes or until golden brown. Repeat until all batter is used. Serve them how you like them, garnished or layered with fresh berries, or topped with sugar free whipped cream.

George's Tips | If you'd like, sprinkle fresh blueberries or sliced strawberries into the pancakes right after pouring into the pan for Blueberry or Strawberry Pancakes. Mixing blueberries right into the batter in the bowl would more than likely turn the batter blue.

Variation | Replacing the sugar substitute with 1 tablespoon of honey will keep things natural and make a pleasantly sweet pancake that's absolutely delicious!

Whole Grain

Christian's Strawberry Banana Muffins

calories: 216 | fat: 13g | protein: 8.5g | fiber: 2.5g | NET CARBS: **16g**

We're always trying to improve upon our recipes, so when we set out to write this book, Christian set out to improve on his favorite Banana Bread Muffins. Now with fresh chopped strawberries, and whole wheat flour for a better texture. Though this is a whole wheat recipe, it's stretched by heart healthy almond flour for less carbs and an added nutty flavor.

Shopping List

nonstick cooking spray
¾ cup **almond flour**
¾ cup **whole wheat flour**
4 large **eggs**
¾ cup **bulk sugar substitute**
2 tablespoons **trans-fat free margarine**, melted
1½ teaspoons **banana extract**
1 teaspoon **baking powder**
¾ cup chopped **strawberries**

1. Place the baking rack in the center of the oven and preheat the oven to 375 degrees. Prepare a 6 cup muffin pan by spraying the cups with nonstick cooking spray, or use a silicone muffin pan for even better results, with muffins that will just pop right out.

2. Mix all of the ingredients, except strawberries, in a bowl with a wooden spoon until well blended. Gently fold strawberries into the batter.

3. Fill the muffin cups with the batter evenly until all has been used.

4. Bake for 20-25 minutes, until the muffin tops turn golden brown and a toothpick stuck into the center comes out clean. Remove the muffins from the oven and let cool for 5 minutes before serving warm or at room temperature.

George's Tips | You can use paper towels to pat the juice off of the strawberries after chopping to keep it from turning your muffin batter too pink. Of course, there's also a lot of strawberry flavor in that juice, so that decision is up to you!

Variation | You can make these gluten free and lower carb by cutting the wheat flour, and doubling the almond flour.

Whole Grain

prep time
5 mins

cook time
40 mins

serves
10-15

Cajun Baked Peanuts

calories: 190 | fat: 16.5g | protein: 8g | fiber: 3g | NET CARBS: 2g

These peanuts are like a crispy roasted version of Southern boiled peanuts… only spicier! When cooked this way, the peanuts will be so crunchy that you can eat them SHELL and all. I love them that way, but they're still quite good out of their shell if you can't bring yourself to do that!

Shopping List

1 large bag **raw peanuts** in shell

¼ cup **vegetable oil**

1 tablespoon **paprika**

½ teaspoon **dry thyme**

½ teaspoon **black pepper**

¼ teaspoon **garlic powder**

¼ teaspoon **cayenne pepper**

2 teaspoons **salt**

1. Preheat the oven to 325 degrees.

2. In a large bowl, combine peanuts in shell and vegetable oil, tossing to coat. In another small bowl, combine remaining ingredients to create the Cajun seasoning.

3. Use a slotted spoon to transfer peanuts from the bowl to a sheet pan, letting some of the oil drip off of them before you transfer. Spread out peanuts on sheet pan in a single layer. Sprinkle all heavily with Cajun seasoning.

4. Bake for 40 minutes, removing the pan and stirring the peanuts around twice. Serve warm or at room temperature.

George's Tips | Raw peanuts are usually sold in big, clear bags near the produce department, right alongside bags of roasted peanuts in shell. Make sure you grab the raw, and not the roasted!

Variation | If you aren't a fan of spicy foods, you can cut out the cayenne pepper, while keeping most of the flavor intact. If you ARE a fan of spicy food, add a pinch of white pepper to the seasoning before baking.

Whole Grain

Crunchy Curried Lentils

calories: 98 | fat: 1g | protein: 6g | fiber: 7.5g | NET CARBS: **7g**

These lentils are a surprising alternative to high fat, high carb crunchy snacks. With loads of protein and fiber, lentils are often considered one of the healthiest foods on the planet. In this recipe they bake into super crunchy little morsels that you can eat by the handful. Just don't eat them too fast, as the curry has a bite to it!

Shopping List

1 cup **dry lentils**
2 teaspoons **canola oil**
1 tablespoon **curry powder**
¾ teaspoon **salt**
½ teaspoon **bulk sugar substitute**, optional

1. Add lentils to a large pot of water over high heat. Cover, bring up to a boil, and then immediately turn heat to low. Simmer lentils on low for 10 minutes.

2. Drain and rinse lentils under cold tap water. Drain very well, letting lentils sit in colander for 5 minutes, shaking occasionally to release any trapped water.

3. Preheat oven to 425 degrees. Pour lentils onto a large sheet pan and cover with remaining ingredients. Use a large spoon to toss all to evenly coat, and then shake pan from side to side to disperse the lentils into a thin layer on the pan. The sugar substitute is optional, but adds a nice touch of sweetness to offset the salt and spicy curry powder.

4. Bake for 25-30 minutes, stirring halfway through, until lentils are very crunchy and have shrunk to nearly half the size they were after boiling. Let cool 5 minutes before eating.

George's Tips | Lentils will get crunchier the more they cool! If storing, leave uncovered to cool for at least 1 hour before covering, so that no moisture gets caught in the container with them.

Variation | If curry isn't your thing, you can also make these similar to my Chilly Weather Chili Chickpeas, recipe page: 36, by tossing the lentils (in step 3) with 2 teaspoons olive oil, 2½ teaspoons chili powder, ½ teaspoon paprika, 1 teaspoon lime juice, and ¾ teaspoon salt.

Whole Grain

Cracked Pepper and Parmesan Popcorn

calories: 120 | fat: 9g | protein: 3.5g | fiber: 1g | NET CARBS: 5g

Christian bought us a microwavable popcorn popper for making our own popcorn without all of the chemicals that they add to store-bought microwave bags. We made up so many varieties, so many times that we literally melted the popper to the inside of our microwave! This recipe was our favorite flavor combination, with a classic stovetop preparation… the way we've gone back to making popcorn!

Shopping List

2 tablespoons **canola oil**
½ cup **popcorn kernels**
2 tablespoons **olive oil**
½ cup **Parmesan cheese**
½ teaspoon **cracked black pepper**

1. Add the oil to a heavy 6 quart pot with lid. Heat for just 1 minute over high heat.

2. Pour popcorn kernels into pot and cover immediately. As the popcorn pops, shake the pan back and forth constantly.

3. When you can hear that the popping has slowed, almost to a stop, remove pot from heat. Carefully open lid (they fly!) and pour popped popcorn into a large serving bowl.

4. Drizzle with olive oil and top with Parmesan and pepper. Toss all to evenly coat. Enjoy!

George's Tips | You may want to add salt to taste, but I don't find that I need any with all of the Parmesan cheese.

Variation | Make this easier and with less fat by using 100% olive oil cooking spray in place of the olive oil. Simply spray the popcorn until the Parmesan and pepper will stick.

Whole Grain

prep time	cook time	serves
10 mins	20 mins	4

Whole Wheat Lo Mein

calories: 265 | fat: 8g | protein: 10g | fiber: 7g | NET CARBS: **30g**

This is my version of the Americanized version of the classic Chinese noodle and vegetable dish we all know as Lo Mein. By replacing the usual starchy white flour or rice noodles with more nutritious whole grain linguine, you digest it slower and you're far less likely to feel hungry again an hour after eating! (I'm sure you've heard that about takeout Chinese food!)

1. Bring a large pot of water to a boil, and cook linguine according to directions on box. Drain and rinse with cold water to stop the cooking process. Set aside.

Shopping List

6 ounces **whole wheat linguine**

2 tablespoons **sesame oil**

½ pound **fresh snow peas**

1 small **red bell pepper**, thinly sliced

8 ounces **mushrooms**, sliced

½ cup **vegetable broth**

¼ cup **reduced sodium teriyaki sauce**

2. Place sesame oil in a large nonstick pan over medium-high heat and heat until almost smoking.

3. Add snow peas and red bell pepper to the pan and sauté 2 minutes before adding the mushrooms. Sauté an additional 2-3 minutes, until vegetables are almost tender.

4. Add vegetable broth and teriyaki sauce, and bring up to a simmer. Once simmering, add the cooked linguine. Toss to combine and sauté an additional 1-2 minutes before serving.

George's Tips | You can use soy sauce in place of teriyaki if that is all that you have on hand. Beef broth can be used in place of the vegetable broth as well. Finally, you can substitute a bag of frozen stir fry vegetables in place of all of the vegetables.

Variation | Start by sautéing thinly sliced chicken breast, top sirloin, or pork, about ⅓ inch thick, before adding the vegetables in step 3 to make a full meal. Sauté just until it lightly browns before adding the vegetables. I also like to add 1 cup of shredded bok choy (a type of cabbage) when adding the linguine in step 4, but you can't always find that at the grocery store, so I've kept the recipe simple.

Whole Grain

Bulgur Wheat and Ground Turkey Stuffed Apples

calories: 290 | fat: 10g | protein: 18g | fiber: 7g | NET CARBS: **26g**

These self contained entrées are great around the holidays, even if you've never heard of bulgur wheat before! Bulgur is just cracked whole wheat, but cooks up a lot like rice or couscous, only better for you, with more fiber.

1. Place 1 cup water in a microwave safe bowl, and microwave 2 minutes or until steaming hot. Add bulgur wheat, stir, and let sit for 15 minutes for all of the water to absorb.

2. While the wheat is sitting, add the margarine to a skillet over medium-high heat. Add the ground turkey and sauté 5 minutes, until it begins to brown. Add the onion, celery salt, cinnamon, ground cloves, and sugar substitute, and continue to sauté an additional 5 minutes. Remove from heat and stir in bulgur wheat.

Shopping List

½ cup **bulgur wheat**

1 tablespoon **trans-fat free margarine**

½ pound **ground turkey**

¼ cup diced **onion**

¼ teaspoon **celery salt**

½ teaspoon **cinnamon**

¼ teaspoon **ground cloves**

2 teaspoons **bulk sugar substitute**

4 green apples

3. Preheat oven to 350 degrees. Slice tops off apples about ¼ inch down, and reserve. Carefully core and hollow out each apple with a paring knife, until the walls are about ½ inch thick.

4. Stuff each hollowed out apple with an even amount of the filling, top with the reserved sliced apple tops, and then place upright in a baking dish. Add 1 cup of hot tap water to the bottom of the baking dish, and cover loosely with tin foil. Bake 30 minutes, and then let cool 5 minutes before serving.

George's Tips | Serve alongside green beans with chopped pecans for a truly festive, and memorable meal!

Variation | If hollowing out apples seems a bit daunting, you can also slice them into wedges and line the bottom of the baking dish (skip the water bath in the dish), and cover with the meat filling. Top with another layer of apple wedges and bake covered with tin foil, to make a casserole version.

Whole Grain

Quinoa Pilaf

calories: 155 | fat: 6g | protein: 6g | fiber: 3g | NET CARBS: 16g

Quinoa may be hard to pronounce (keen-wah) but it's definitely easier to cook than you'd think! This rice and pasta free pilaf is not only a good, whole grain carb, but also gluten free! With quinoa being higher in fiber and tremendously higher in protein than rice, this pilaf is as nutritious as it is delicious.

1. Thoroughly rinse quinoa in a fine mesh strainer or by hand in a large bowl of water.

2. Add 1 tablespoon of the margarine to a medium sized pot on the stove over medium-high heat and cook until melted. Add celery and onion to pot and sauté 3 minutes or until celery begins to turn translucent, then transfer to a small bowl and set aside.

Shopping List

1 cup **dry quinoa**
2 tablespoons **trans-fat free margarine**
½ cup chopped **celery**
¼ cup minced **yellow onion**
2 cups **chicken broth**
½ teaspoon **poultry seasoning**
1 tablespoon chopped **parsley** (or **2** teaspoons **parsley flakes**)

3. Place pot back onto the heat and add the remaining tablespoon of margarine and rinsed quinoa. Cook quinoa and margarine, stirring constantly, 2 minutes before pouring in the chicken broth and poultry seasoning.

4. Bring to a boil, then reduce heat to low, cover pot and simmer for 10 minutes.

5. Stir in the cooked celery and onion mixture, and parsley. Recover pot and cook an additional 5 minutes before fluffing with a spoon, and serving hot.

George's Tips | Quinoa is so small that it can be tremendously difficult to rinse. I've found that the best way to do this is to swirl it around in a large bowl of water with your hands. Getting it out of the bowl can be tricky, but scooping it out against the wall of the bowl is easiest.

Variation | I like to add a handful of chopped pistachios to my pilaf just before serving. Slivered almonds go great as well!

Whole Grain

prep time	cook time	yield	serves
15 mins	25 mins	6 muffins	6

Bran Muffins

calories: 125 | fat: 5g | protein: 5g | fiber: 5.5g | NET CARBS: **12.5g**

Wheat bran is about as high in fiber as you get, which can help keep your body from digesting the carbs around it … so while these muffins might seem a little higher in carbs than others in this book, they are most definitely good for you. And without a doubt, they are most definitely good muffins too! Just slice in half, spread a little trans-fat free margarine on them and grill to make them even better!

Shopping List

¾ cup **wheat bran**

⅔ cup **whole wheat flour**

⅔ cup **unsweetened soy milk**

2 tablespoons **trans-fat free margarine**, melted

whites of **2** large **eggs**

⅔ cup **bulk sugar substitute**

½ teaspoon **vanilla extract**

1 teaspoon **baking powder**

¾ teaspoon **ground cinnamon**

1. Place the baking rack in the center of the oven and preheat the oven to 350 degrees. Line a 6 cup muffin pan with paper muffin cups, or use an unlined silicone muffin pan for even better results.

2. Mix all of the ingredients in a bowl with a wooden spoon until well blended. Fill the muffin cups with the batter evenly until all has been used.

3. Bake for 20-25 minutes, until the muffin tops turn golden brown and a toothpick stuck into the center comes out clean.

4. Remove the muffins from the oven and let cool for 5 minutes before serving warm or at room temperature.

George's Tips | These muffins are quite large, so you may want to spread out into 8 muffin cups, just make sure you keep an eye on them, as they will cook faster!

Variation | Try adding ½ cup of fresh blueberries to the batter for Blueberry Bran Muffins that are out of this world! Or try the same with raspberries.

Whole Grain

Desserts

Strawberry Dreams

calories: 50 | fat: 4g | protein: 1g | fiber: 0g | NET CARBS: **2g**

I just made another batch of these cream stuffed Strawberry Dreams using strawberries from Rachel's garden; now I've got to dream up some kind of way to STOP eating them. This is one of those catch 22 recipes for me, because you can pop them in your mouth as fast as you can make them!

Shopping List

½ cup **heavy cream**
¼ cup **bulk sugar substitute**
½ teaspoon **vanilla extract**
4 ounces **light cream cheese**, softened
12 large **strawberries**, about **1** quart

1. With an electric mixer on high, whip the cream just until frothy. Add the sugar substitute and vanilla extract. Whip on high speed until soft peaks form.

2. Add the softened cream cheese and whip for a few seconds more to combine. Be careful not to overwhip, or the whipped cream will break down. Place the mixture into a pastry bag.

3. Cut a deep criss-cross notch in the bottom of each strawberry and place them leafy top down on a plate. Slightly spread open the cut end and use the pastry bag to pipe a dollop of the cream mixture into the notch. Serve garnished with a single fresh mint leaf on each, if desired.

George's Tips | Use a wide star tip for the pastry bag. If you do not have a pastry bag, you can simply fill up a plastic food storage bag, seal, and cut the tip of one corner off to make one.

Variation | Make savory appetizer versions by using less sugar substitute and adding 1 tablespoon fresh chopped basil, and a dash of cracked black pepper!

Desserts

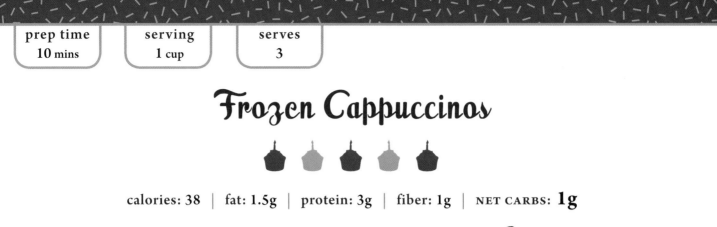

prep time 10 mins	serving 1 cup	serves 3

Frozen Cappuccinos

calories: 38 | fat: 1.5g | protein: 3g | fiber: 1g | NET CARBS: **1g**

I don't think anyone would argue with me if I said that making your own frozen blended coffee drinks can save you money! The other great thing is, making them yourself can also save you from a ton of sugar that you'd get in a coffeehouse. Soy milk works great in these as well, as it is thick and creamy like heavy cream without nearly as much fat, but most importantly, it doesn't whip into whipped cream in the middle of blending your drink! (This happened to me with heavy cream.)

Shopping List

½ cup strong **coffee**, chilled

1 cup **unsweetened soy milk**

2 teaspoons **vanilla extract**

2-3 tablespoons **bulk sugar substitute**

1. Add all ingredients to a blender and cover with 1½ cups ice. As the final drink will depend on the strength of your coffee, start with 2 tablespoons of bulk sugar substitute and add more after blending, until you get it to your liking.

2. Blend together until ice has been chopped fine and dispersed throughout. Taste for sweetness and add sweetener, if desired. Serve immediately, topped with sugar free whipped cream!

George's Tips | To make strong coffee, simply add 2-3 extra scoops of grounds to your coffeemaker when brewing a pot. I like to make this with ¼ cup of espresso.

Variation | You can also make this with instant coffee granules instead of brewed. Simply add 2½ teaspoons and up the soy milk by ½ cup.

prep time	cook time	chill time	serves
10 mins	30 mins	2.5 hrs	4

Fool Proof Lemon Curd Custard

calories: 165 | fat: 13g | protein: 7g | fiber: 0g | NET CARBS: **6.5g**

Traditional English lemon curd is typically cooked on top of the stove. It takes a whole lot of stirring and sometimes it just plain curdles more than it's supposed to! This quick and easy method is simple and works every time.

Shopping List

nonstick cooking spray
2 whole large **eggs** +2 **egg yolks**
¾ cup **bulk sugar substitute**
1¼ cups **half and half**
2 teaspoons **lemon zest**
⅓ cup fresh **lemon juice**

1. Place the oven rack in the center position, and make a water bath by filling a shallow roasting pan with about 1 inch of water. Place roasting pan on center rack and preheat oven to 375 degrees. Spray four 6 ounce custard cups or ramekins with nonstick cooking spray.

2. Add eggs, egg yolks, sugar substitute, and half and half to a blender and blend 30 seconds, until smooth.

3. Add lemon zest and lemon juice, and blend on low for 15 seconds, just until combined.

4. Fill each greased custard cup with equal amounts of the mixture.

5. Place the filled dishes in the preheated water bath and bake for about 30 minutes, or until a crust forms on top and the center feels firm to the touch. Remove from the oven and water bath, and then let cool on the counter for 30 minutes, followed by 2 hours in the refrigerator. Serve chilled with fresh berries, if desired.

George's Tips | When pouring the mixture into the cups in step 4, it's best to equally disperse the mixture in 2-3 rounds, filling a little in each cup, each round. This way each cup gets an equal amount of the lemon zest that tends to settle at the bottom of the blender.

Variation | Substitute 1¼ cups unsweetened soy milk in place of the half and half to lower the fat in this recipe. You can also substitute 3 teaspoons orange zest in place of the lemon zest and replace the lemon juice with 2 teaspoons of vanilla extract for an Oranges and Cream Custard.

Desserts

prep time	cook time	yield	serves
25 mins	40 mins	25 squares	25

Flourless Fudge Brownies

calories: 100 | fat: 9g | protein: 3.5g | fiber: 3g | NET CARBS: **1.5g**

These brownies require a little more prep work than most of the recipes in this book, but it isn't a bad tradeoff when you consider that you don't add a drop of flour or sugar to make them. Instead of flour we've used amazingly heart healthy and high fiber flax seed, which also adds its own nutty taste.

Shopping List

nonstick cooking spray

½ cup **half and half**

4 ounces **unsweetened baking chocolate**, chopped

8 tablespoons **trans-fat free margarine**

2 cups **bulk sugar substitute**

1 tablespoon **vanilla extract**

5 large **eggs**

¼ cup **unsweetened cocoa powder**

1½ cups **milled flax seed**

2 teaspoons **baking powder**

1. Place oven rack in the center position and preheat to 350 degrees. Spray an 8x8 baking dish with nonstick cooking spray.

2. Fill a pot with 2 inches of water and place over medium-high heat, bringing water to a very low simmer. Place a stainless steel bowl over the pot (above the water) to create a double boiler.

3. Add ¼ cup of the half and half, and all of the baking chocolate to the stainless steel bowl, mixing with a rubber spatula for about 2 minutes, until chocolate is melted and mixture is creamy. Set aside to cool down.

4. Place margarine in an electric mixer on high speed and beat until fluffy, about 2-3 minutes. Add sugar substitute, vanilla extract, and remaining half and half, and then continue beating as you add the eggs, one at a time.

5. Stop the mixer and add the cocoa powder, milled flax seed, baking powder, melted baking chocolate mixture, and ¼ cup of tap water. Restart the mixer on low and mix well, about another 2 minutes.

6. Spread in greased baking dish and bake 35-40 minutes or until tapping on the center with a wooden spoon feels springy. Cool on a wire rack for 10-15 minutes before refrigerating for 2 hours for the best flavor and a more solid, fudge-like consistency.

George's Tips | The batter will look gritty, but that is completely normal.

Variation | Add ½ cup chopped walnuts to the batter before baking to make Walnut Fudge Brownies.

Raspberry Cream Fool Parfaits

calories: 80 | fat: 7g | protein: 0.5g | fiber: 1g | NET CARBS: **2g**

This old fashioned British dessert is a whole lot like a mousse, only made in two parts: the whipped cream, and the raspberry puree. Once folded together, you are fooled! Actually, I'm not sure why they named it this, but I've got to have at least one more bad pun in me about it... I mean, I'd be a fool to waste such an opportunity!

Shopping List

1 cup **frozen raspberries**, thawed

⅓ cup + **2** tablespoons **bulk sugar substitute**

1 cup **heavy cream**

1 teaspoon **vanilla extract**

1. Using a blender or food processor, puree raspberries with the 2 tablespoons of sugar substitute, until smooth.

2. With an electric mixer on high, whip the cream just until frothy. Add the sugar substitute, and vanilla extract. Whip on high speed until soft peaks form. Be careful not to overwhip, or the whipped cream will break down.

3. Use a spoon to mix in the raspberry puree, leaving visible streaks of red with peaks of white. Spoon into parfait glasses and serve chilled. Garnish with fresh or frozen raspberries and mint, if desired.

George's Tips | Don't be a "fool" and let these sit around—the sooner you eat them the better, as real whipped cream quickly breaks down over time.

Variation | Use strawberries if you don't have raspberries, and top with cocoa powder mixed with a little sugar substitute for added decadence! Or use almond extract in place of the vanilla and add ¼ cup of ricotta sweetened with 2 tablespoons sugar substitute instead of the berries for cannoli parfaits!

Desserts

Dark Chocolate Peanut Butter Cups

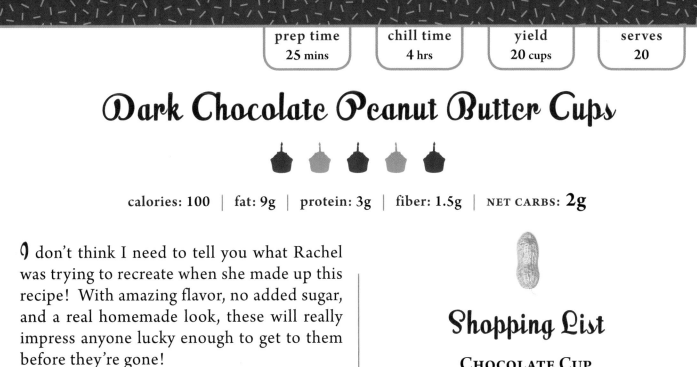

calories: 100 | fat: 9g | protein: 3g | fiber: 1.5g | NET CARBS: 2g

I don't think I need to tell you what Rachel was trying to recreate when she made up this recipe! With amazing flavor, no added sugar, and a real homemade look, these will really impress anyone lucky enough to get to them before they're gone!

Shopping List

CHOCOLATE CUP

4 tablespoons **trans-fat free margarine**

1½ cups **bulk sugar substitute**

2 tablespoons **half and half**

4 ounces **unsweetened baking chocolate**, chopped

PEANUT BUTTER FILLING

½ cup **almond flour**

½ cup **bulk sugar substitute**

½ cup **natural peanut butter**

1. Arrange 20 mini paper cupcake liners in mini muffin pans, on a sheet pan or in a large rectangular baking dish.

2. Fill a pot with 2 inches of water and place over medium-high heat, bringing water to a very low simmer. Place a stainless steel bowl over the pot (above the water) to create a double boiler.

3. Add the margarine, sugar substitute, and half and half to the stainless steel bowl, mixing with a rubber spatula until margarine is melted and well combined.

4. Add the chopped unsweetened chocolate and slowly stir for about 2 minutes, just until melted and combined with the liquid. Remove from heat and pour an equal amount into each of the 20 cupcake liners, filling about half way.

5. In a mixing bowl, combine all Peanut Butter Filling ingredients, mixing well. If peanut butter is very thick to begin with, thin filling only slightly with 1-2 tablespoons of half and half.

6. Form filling into 20 equal sized balls and push into the chocolate in the cupcake liners. Flatten down with your fingers or a spoon. Refrigerate for at least 4 hours, or until firm.

George's Tips | We didn't have any mini muffin pans to form these in, so we doubled up on the paper liners, using 2 per cup to give added support. We also let them refrigerate for 20 minutes and then pressed the sides of the cups up more as the chocolate was cooler and more moldable.

Variation | These are so good that we've never made any variations on it, but I don't see why you couldn't make it with natural cashew butter!

Cheesecake Squares

calories: **155** | fat: **14g** | protein: **5g** | fiber: **1g** | NET CARBS: **1.5g**

My Stella Style New York Ricotta Cheesecake is most definitely my signature recipe. Rachel and I have made many variations on it over the years, but this time I gave Rachel a pretty tall order: make it easier and make it in less than the original 4 hours in the oven! We found that spreading them out into bars and removing the ricotta kept all of the flavor intact, while cutting the oven time down to just 45 minutes!

1. Place oven rack in center position and preheat oven to 350 degrees. Spray an 8x8 baking dish with nonstick cooking spray.

2. In a large bowl, combine all Crust ingredients and mix well. Pour into greased dish, spreading evenly, and bake on the center rack for 15 minutes, or until lightly browned. Let cool 5 minutes after baking.

Shopping List

nonstick cooking spray

CRUST

2 large **eggs**, beaten until frothy

1 cup **almond flour**

⅓ cup **bulk sugar substitute**

1 teaspoon **baking powder**

FILLING

16 ounces **cream cheese**, softened

½ cup **bulk sugar substitute**

1 tablespoon **vanilla extract**

3 large **eggs**

3. While crust bakes, prepare the cheesecake filling by beating cream cheese, sugar substitute, and vanilla extract in a mixer on medium speed until combined. Add eggs and continue mixing on medium, just until mixed and smooth.

4. Pour filling over crust, spread evenly, and bake in the 350 degree oven for 30 minutes, or until center is set and a toothpick inserted into the center comes out mostly clean.

5. Cool on a wire rack for 30 minutes and then refrigerate for at least 2 hours before cutting into 16 squares to serve.

Variation | Prepare in an 8 inch springform pan to make a traditionally shaped cheesecake, though this may add a few minutes baking to properly set in step 4. Make an apple cinnamon topping to top the squares or cheesecake previously mentioned by combining 3 cups of peeled and thinly sliced apple slices, ¼ cup bulk sugar substitute, ¼ teaspoon ground cinnamon, and ¼ cup chopped walnuts. Carefully spread over filling in step 4 and lengthen baking time by 5-10 minutes to properly set.

Desserts

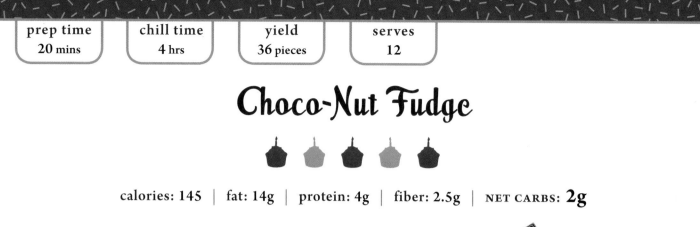

prep time	chill time	yield	serves
20 mins	4 hrs	36 pieces	12

Choco-Nut Fudge

calories: 145 | fat: 14g | protein: 4g | fiber: 2.5g | NET CARBS: **2g**

This fudge, made without adding any sugar, is rich and chocolaty and a great fix (or gift!) for a major sweet tooth. Sadly, I can't take any of the credit for this one (or most of the dessert recipes in this book) as Rachel is the baker of the family.

1. Line a 9x5 or similar loaf pan with aluminum foil.

2. Fill a pot with 2 inches of water and place over medium-high heat, bringing water to a very low simmer. Place a stainless steel bowl over the pot (above the water) to create a double boiler.

Shopping List

4 tablespoons **trans-fat free margarine**

1½ cups **bulk sugar substitute**

2 tablespoons **half and half**

4 ounces **unsweetened baking chocolate**, chopped

1 tablespoon **vanilla extract**

1 cup **chopped walnuts**

3. Add the margarine, sugar substitute, and half and half to the stainless steel bowl, mixing with a rubber spatula until margarine is melted and well combined.

4. Add the chopped unsweetened chocolate and slowly stir for about 2 minutes, just until melted and combined with the liquid.

5. Remove from heat and stir in vanilla and chopped walnuts. Pour into aluminum foil lined loaf pan and refrigerate at least 4 hours, until firm. Cut into 36 small squares to serve.

George's Tips | We only use "Baker's" brand unsweetened chocolate squares to make our chocolate desserts. It just seems to melt the best.

Variation | Chopped pecans, cashews, peanuts, hazelnuts or almonds can be used in place of the walnuts. My favorite are the hazelnuts, but you will most likely have to chop them yourself, as they usually don't sell them in bags.

Desserts

Soda Fountain Vanilla Egg Creams

calories: 50 | fat: 3.5g | protein: 1g | fiber: 0g | NET CARBS: **2g**

Though you may have never heard of an egg cream, I can assure you that there are no eggs involved in this old fashioned soda fountain drink that originated in New York! Similar to an ice cream float, without the ice cream, this creamy homemade soda is best ice cold, with a foamy head similar to a beer.

Shopping List

1 teaspoon **vanilla extract**
3 teaspoons **bulk sugar substitute**
2 tablespoons **half and half**
1¼ cups **club soda**

1. Place vanilla extract, sugar substitute, and half and half in a tall 12 ounce glass. Use a long spoon to mix well.

2. Slowly pour club soda into glass, pouring it against the side of the glass to create the most foam. Stop when the foam reaches the top of the glass. Repeat for more servings or just enjoy!

George's Tips | It's very important to use ice cold club soda, and almost as important to use a new bottle or can, as you'll want this really carbonated to make it extra foamy.

Variation | This can be made with much less fat by using 3 tablespoons of unsweetened soy milk in place of the 2 tablespoons of half and half. Replace the club soda with diet cola or diet root beer and cut the sugar substitute down to 1 teaspoon to make a quick "ice cream float" without any ice cream at all.

Drunken Melon Sorbet

calories: 80 | fat: 0g | protein: 1g | fiber: 2g | NET CARBS: **12g**

This white wine and melon sorbet is the perfect ending to a dinner party with friends. Made with either cantaloupe or honeydew, I highly suggest whipping up a batch of each and pairing a scoop of both in a wine glass, garnished with fresh berries.

Shopping List

2 cups chopped **cantaloupe** or **honeydew** flesh

⅓ cup **dry white wine**

¼ cup **bulk sugar substitute**

1. Place all ingredients in the bowl of a food processor and blend until smooth. Depending on the ripeness of the melon and the power of the food processor, you may need to add 1-2 tablespoons of water to get the mixture to properly blend.

2. Transfer to a covered container and freeze for 2-3 hours, or until hard.

3. Serve directly from the freezer for a texture that is more similar to Italian ice, or if you have a strong food processor, scoop the sorbet back into the processor by the spoonful and blend an additional time before serving for the smoothest consistency.

George's Tips | Freeze the sorbet in individual serving dishes for even easier serving once frozen. Though this recipe is easily doubled or tripled for more than 2 servings, I suggest blending the batches separately as food processors just work better with less in them.

Variation | Water and a teaspoon of lemon juice can be substituted for the white wine, though the alcohol in the wine resists freezing, helping the sorbet stay creamier without the use of an ice cream maker. Substituting water and lemon juice will result in more of an Italian ice style texture.

Buttercream Cheese Frosting

calories: 75 | fat: 7g | protein: 2g | fiber: 0g | NET CARBS: **1.5g**

I think everyone would attest to the fact that buttercream frosting is delicious, but up until now we have never even attempted to make anything even similar to it as you need pretty much an entire box of confectioner's sugar to get the consistency right. We've found that the best way to make it without sugar is to replace the missing bulk from the sugar with cream cheese, which creates a delicious hybrid between buttercream and cream cheese frosting. Then believe it or not, we found that using trans-fat free margarine (something we've been using to eat healthier) whipped into a better frosting texture than actual butter!

Shopping List

4 tablespoons **trans-fat free margarine**

8 ounces **reduced fat cream cheese**

¾ cup **bulk sugar substitute**

1 teaspoon **vanilla extract**

1. Allow margarine and cream cheese to soften to almost room temperature before using.

2. Beat all ingredients in an electric mixer on high until well combined and light and fluffy.

3. Spread on a completely cooled cake.

George's Tips | It should go without saying that you can use this frosting to frost a White Birthday Cake, recipe page: 203. This also goes great as a topping on a batch of Flourless Fudge Brownies, recipe page: 183.

Variation | Add 3 tablespoons of unsweetened cocoa powder (we like Hershey's brand) and ¼ cup more bulk sugar substitute to turn this into a Chocolate Frosting.

Pumpkin Flan Minis

calories: 140 | fat: 10g | protein: 6.5g | fiber: 1.5g | NET CARBS: **5g**

Pumpkin is one of our favorite dessert staples, as it keeps desserts moist and delicious in much the same way that brown sugar would, without having to add any sugar at all. Available canned all year round, you definitely don't have to saw into a pumpkin to make something delicious like these personal sized flan cups.

Shopping List

nonstick cooking spray
3 eggs
⅔ cup **canned pumpkin**
1 cup **half and half**
½ teaspoon **ground cinnamon**
1 teaspoon **vanilla extract**
⅓ cup **bulk sugar substitute**

1. Place the oven rack in the center position and make a water bath by filling a shallow roasting pan with about 1 inch of water. Place roasting pan on center rack and preheat oven to 350 degrees. Spray four 6 ounce custard cups or ramekins with nonstick cooking spray.

2. Add eggs to a large bowl and whisk until frothy. Add remaining ingredients and mix until well combined.

3. Evenly pour mixture into the greased cups. Place cups into the preheated water bath in oven and bake for 45 minutes or until solid. A toothpick inserted into the center should come out mostly clean.

4. Let cool for 30 minutes on counter before refrigerating for at least 2 hours and serving cold. Serve topped with sugar-free whipped cream, if you desire.

George's Tips | When shopping for canned pumpkin, be sure to purchase 100% pure pumpkin and not pumpkin pie filling, which is filled with added sugar.

Variation | For even more of a pumpkin pie flavor, simply replace the cinnamon with ½ teaspoon of pumpkin pie spice.

Desserts

prep time	cook time	yield	serves
5 mins	10 mins	16 cookies	8

Pecan Sandy Meltaways

calories: 170 | fat: 15.5g | protein: 4.5g | fiber: 1.5g | NET CARBS: **3g**

Pecan Sandies have long been a favorite of mine, and I don't even know why. They're quite... sandy... when you think about it. While I can't promise that my version of my old favorite is anywhere near as sandy as a store bought (overly processed) cookie, I can promise that mine are sugar and flour free!

1. Preheat oven to 375 degrees and line a sheet pan with parchment paper.

2. Using a stand or hand held mixer, add the cream cheese, margarine, sugar substitute, egg and vanilla to the mixing bowl and beat on high until creamy and fluffy.

Shopping List

2 ounces **light cream cheese**, softened

2 tablespoons **trans-fat free margarine**

1 cup **bulk sugar substitute**

1 large **egg**

1 teaspoon **vanilla extract**

1 cup **almond flour**

½ teaspoon **baking soda**

¼ teaspoon **salt**

2 ounces **chopped pecans**

3. Add in the remaining ingredients and mix on medium until well blended.

4. Using a teaspoon or 1 ounce ice cream scoop, drop 16 evenly spaced cookies on the lined pan and bake for about 8-10 minutes. Let cool 10-15 minutes before serving.

George's Tips | You can press the cookies down into the parchment paper a little before baking for a crispier cookie.

Variation | This basic cookie dough can be used to make many varieties of cookies. Try adding ½ teaspoon cinnamon or ginger for a refreshing crisp, or replace the pecans with almond slices and add dry coconut!

Desserts

Lip Smacking Lemon Bars

calories: 90 | fat: 7g | protein: 5g | fiber: 1g | NET CARBS: **2g**

Writing this book has been an enlightening experience for me, as I didn't even know I could make a dessert like this so simply! With only 6 unique ingredients, these sugarless, flourless cake bars are tart and sweet, and we've made them twice this week alone.

1. Preheat oven to 350 degrees, and spray an 8x8 baking dish with nonstick cooking spray.

2. In a large bowl, combine all Cake ingredients, and mix well. Pour into prepared pan, and bake on the center rack for 15 minutes, or until lightly browned.

3. While the cake bakes, prepare the Lemon Glaze by whisking all ingredients together in a bowl.

Shopping List

nonstick cooking spray

CAKE

2 large **eggs**, beaten until frothy

1¼ cups **almond flour**

⅓ cup **bulk sugar substitute**

1 teaspoon **baking powder**

BAKED LEMON GLAZE

3 large **eggs**, beaten until frothy

1 cup **bulk sugar substitute**

1 teaspoon **lemon zest**

¼ cup fresh **lemon juice**

½ teaspoon **baking powder**

4. Remove browned cake from oven and let rest for 5 minutes. Pour the glaze over it while still hot, and bake for an additional 20 minutes or until firm. Refrigerate for at least 2 hours to serve chilled, cut into 12 bars.

George's Tips | Sprinkle with a pinch of sugar substitute before serving for a powdered sugar like dusting. Top that with some sugar-free apricot preserves, just because that sounds really good to me right now!

Variation | The cake in this recipe may be used as a base for most any of your favorites. Try adding ½ cup of shelled walnut halves to the cake, and topping with a cinnamon flavored glaze made by skipping the lemon ingredients and replacing them with 1 teaspoon ground cinnamon.

Desserts

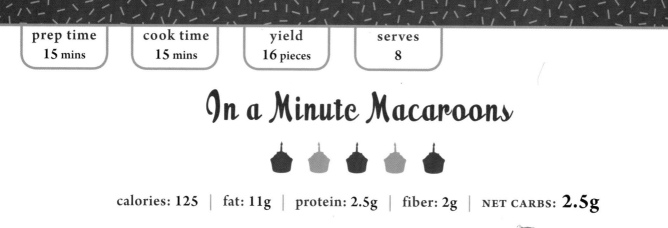

prep time 15 mins	cook time 15 mins	yield 16 pieces	serves 8

In a Minute Macaroons

calories: 125 | fat: 11g | protein: 2.5g | fiber: 2g | NET CARBS: **2.5g**

Okay, so maybe these coconut macaroons aren't really made in only a minute, but they're about as close to that as you can get! That's one of the reasons why macaroons are a preferred dessert recipe for chefs (that aren't married to Rachel)... chefs are notoriously bad at baking, but macaroons are easy and almost always come out great!

Shopping List

3 egg whites
1½ teaspoons **vanilla extract**
½ cup **bulk sugar substitute**
1 tablespoon **trans-fat free margarine,** melted
½ teaspoon **baking soda**
1½ packed cups **unsweetened shredded coconut**

1. Place oven rack in the center position and preheat to 350 degrees. Line a baking sheet with parchment paper.

2. In a large bowl, beat egg whites and vanilla extract until frothy. Stir in sugar substitute, margarine, and baking soda.

3. Fold coconut into the wet ingredients until well combined.

4. Wet fingers to prevent sticking, form the mixture into 16 equal balls about 4 teaspoons in size, and place on the lined baking sheet.

5. Bake for 15 minutes or until they begin to turn golden brown all over. Let cool 15 minutes before serving.

George's Tips | Pack the dough into a 1 ounce ice cream scoop to form perfectly circular macaroons. You can also bake them in paper mini muffin liners for a really nice presentation.

Variation | Make almond macaroons by replacing the vanilla extract with 1 teaspoon of almond extract and pressing 1 whole raw almond into the top of each macaroon before baking.

Desserts

prep time	chill time	serves
20 mins	4 hrs	8

No-Bake Peanut Butter Cheesecake

calories: 350 | fat: 27g | protein: 10g | fiber: 1.5g | NET CARBS: **8g**

The first sugar free cheesecake Rachel and I ever made was a no-bake cheesecake like this one and we enjoyed it through many of our first months of weight loss before we ever tried to actually bake a cheesecake. While our baked cheesecakes might have gotten me my own show on the Food Network, it's sometimes easy to forget that no-bakes can be delicious too—and easier to make!

Shopping List

½ cup chopped **peanuts**
1 envelope **unflavored gelatin**
16 ounces **cream cheese**
½ cup **natural peanut butter**
1 cup **bulk sugar substitute**
1 tablespoon **vanilla extract**

1. Sprinkle the chopped peanuts evenly over the bottom of an 8 inch pie or cake pan. Place a small pot with ¾ of a cup of water on the stove to boil. Place another ¼ cup of cold water in a mixing bowl.

2. Sprinkle gelatin over cold water in the mixing bowl and let sit for 1 minute to "bloom" before stirring in the boiling water until completely dissolved.

3. Using an electric mixer on medium, beat cream cheese, peanut butter, sugar substitute, and vanilla extract just until combined. Set the electric mixer to high and slowly pour the hot gelatin mixture into the cheesecake filling, beating until all is combined.

4. Pour the cheesecake filling over the chopped peanuts in the pie or cake pan, shaking from side to side to settle any air bubbles. Refrigerate for 3-4 hours until firm. Cut into 8 slices and serve topped with additional chopped peanuts and whipped cream.

George's Tips | It's best to let the cream cheese soften on the counter for about 30 minutes before starting, as the colder the cheesecake filling is before introducing the gelatin, the greater your chances of the gelatin hardening and creating lumps before it is evenly mixed.

Variation | You can significantly cut down the fat in this recipe by using reduced fat cream cheese in place of the regular cream cheese. You'll get a slightly better texture with regular, but you won't lose any of the flavor by making the switch.

Desserts

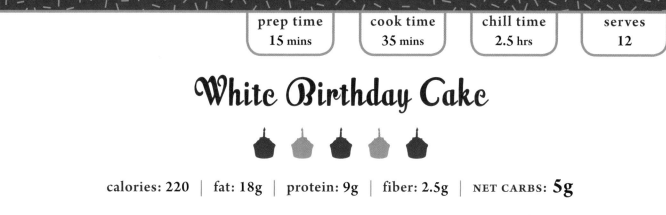

prep time	cook time	chill time	serves
15 mins	35 mins	2.5 hrs	12

White Birthday Cake

calories: 220 | fat: 18g | protein: 9g | fiber: 2.5g | NET CARBS: **5g**

Rachel has attempted many birthday cakes for our sons and myself over the years (and I've attempted one gigantic failure of a birthday cake for Rachel), but none of them have ever come close to this brand new recipe she came up with for a super moist white cake without using any flour or sugar.

1. Place oven rack in the center position and preheat to 350 degrees. Spray an 8 inch round cake pan with nonstick cooking spray, and sprinkle 1 tablespoon bulk sugar substitute around the bottom and edges.

2. In a large bowl, beat eggs until frothy. Add vanilla extract and ¼ cup of tap water to the bowl and beat to combine.

Shopping List

nonstick cooking spray

¾ cup + **1** tablespoon **bulk sugar substitute**

5 eggs

1 tablespoon **vanilla extract**

2½ cups **almond flour**, made from blanched almonds

1 tablespoon **baking powder**

1 batch **Buttercream Cheese Frosting**, recipe page: **194**

3. In a medium bowl, mix the almond flour, remaining ¾ cup sugar substitute, and baking powder, then beat this dry ingredient mixture into the wet ingredient mixture until all are combined.

4. Pour the finished batter into the prepared cake pan and bake 30-35 minutes, or until center is firm and springy. A toothpick inserted into the center should come out mostly clean.

5. Cool on a wire rack for 30 minutes before refrigerating for at least 2 hours. Turn pan upside down and shake to release cake. Frost with the Buttercream Cheese Frosting, cut into 12 slices and serve.

Note: | Nutrition facts for this recipe already include the amounts for the frosting.

Variation | While you could double the recipe to make a two layer cake, almond flour is very filling and satisfying, so we simply cut the one layer of this recipe in half horizontally using a long bread knife to make two layers.

About the Book

The nutritional information and calorie counts on the recipes in this book were compiled from reputable sources to the best of our ability. Counts may differ, depending on the specific brands of ingredients you purchase. Carbohydrate counts especially differ from brand to brand, so always read the label! Variations, or suggestions for garnish are not included in the nutritional information.

Net carbohydrate counts shown in this book were figured by subtracting fiber grams from the total carbohydrate count, as the fiber does not absorb into the body. Fiber carbs are the ONLY type that we subtract. Net carbs were rounded to the nearest .5 of a gram.

All food photographs were taken in the Stella home by Christian and his wife Elise, with food cooked and plated by George and Rachel. All photographs are of REAL food, really made from the recipes and then really eaten, really fast. All fresh herbs and some vegetables in photographs were grown in Rachel's garden.

RECIPE INDEX

Seafood

Slow Cooker Cookery

Vegetables and Sides

Wholesome Whole Grains...

Desserts

George Stella has been a professional chef for more than 25 years. He has appeared on numerous television and news shows, including two seasons of his own show, *Low Carb and Lovin' It* on the Food Network. He is also an official spokesman for the Junior Leagues' *Kids in the Kitchen* initiative to empower youth to make healthy lifestyle choices. Connecticut born, he's spent more than half of his life in Florida, where he lives today with his wife Rachel. This is his fourth cookbook.